1.90 (Title II) ERS 9-66 (Sweaningen)

THE HOME UNIVERSITY LIBRARY
OF MODERN KNOWLEDGE

193

THE CIVILIZATION
OF SPAIN

The Civilization of Spain

J. B. TREND

EMERITUS PROFESSOR OF SPANISH IN THE
UNIVERSITY OF CAMBRIDGE
MEMBER OF THE HISPANIC SOCIETY OF AMERICA

LONDON
OXFORD UNIVERSITY PRESS
NEW YORK   TORONTO

Oxford University Press, Amen House, London E.C.4

GLASGOW NEW YORK TORONTO MELBOURNE WELLINGTON
BOMBAY CALCUTTA MADRAS KARACHI LAHORE DACCA
CAPE TOWN SALISBURY NAIROBI IBADAN ACCRA
KUALA LUMPUR HONG KONG

First edition 1944
Reprinted 1944, 1946, 1949, 1952, 1958, 1960 *and* 1963

PRINTED IN GREAT BRITAIN

17893

CONTENTS

MAPS

The poem on page 178 is reproduced by courtesy of The Dolphin Book Co. Ltd. from 'Poems' by F. Garcia Lorca, translated by Stephen Spender and J. L. Gili (London, 1942).

CHAPTER I
THE DISCOVERY OF SPAIN

SPAIN, which was to play so great a part in the discovery and colonization of the New World, was once discovered and colonized itself.

Phoenicians had been to Spain soon after the siege of Troy; later, they had even sailed out into the Atlantic and founded a trading-post at Gades (Cadiz) at a time when a voyage to Spain was as great an adventure as the voyage of Ulysses. The Phoenicians were not so much colonists and settlers as merchants and seamen. Like many European business men in later times, interested in the development of Spain and Spanish America, their chief concern was with mining. It was they who in ages already remote had found sailors ready to venture out of the Mediterranean, even further than Cadiz, to the lands where the summer nights were shorter, to fetch tin from the mines in Cornwall—the Cassiterides. Cornish tin and Spanish copper made bronze. It was the Bronze Age; and as early as the eighth century B.C. the Phoenicians were buying the copper of Río Tinto. They also salted Spanish fish and dyed Spanish wool with the purple of Tyre, brought from the other end of the Mediterranean; and, as Herodotus tells us, they provided Spanish esparto-grass for the ropes used in Xerxes' bridge across the Hellespont, in 481 B.C. They, and their African colonists the Carthaginians, held the naval and commercial hegemony of the Far West from the eighth to the third centuries B.C. Beyond the Pillars of Hercules (the Straits of Gibraltar) the sea could not be crossed or sounded, Plato says, because of the thick mud which came up from the sunken island of Atlantis. Yarns like these, and the tales of the Sargasso weed choking the same waters, or of the sea-monsters which infested them, were probably put about by the Phoenicians and Carthaginians to keep the Greeks away.

If the Phoenicians were the first to discover Spain, the first to write about it were the Greeks. Homer knew the sound of the west wind as it blew in steadily from the ocean outside the Pillars of Hercules; Hesiod, whose brother was a sailor, had heard of the golden apples of the Hesperides—perhaps nuggets of the Spanish gold which the Phoenicians mixed with silver to make *elektron*. The first Greek discoverers of Spain were Ionians. Herodotus describes how a ship from Samos, sailing to Egypt (her captain was Colaeus), was driven out of her course and carried right past the Pillars to Tartēssos (the Tarshish of the Bible, somewhere in southern Spain), at that time a virgin port which no Greek had ever visited (*c.* 630 B.C.): 'The Samians brought back greater profits than any Greeks of whom we have record.'

The earliest Greeks to make long voyages deliberately were the Phocaeans. They reached Tartēssos in the sixth century B.C., sailing not in merchant ships but in penteconters, fifty-oared men-of-war. They made friends with the king of the Tartessians, Arganthonius, who (it is recorded) ruled Tartēssos for eighty years and lived to be one hundred and twenty. He first entreated them to leave Ionia and stay in Spain; and then, when he could not persuade them to do that, and learnt from them how the Persian power was increasing, he gave them money to build a wall round their city. But in 540 Phocaea fell to the Persians, and a group of Phocaeans sailed for Spain as refugees. They may be regarded as the first Pilgrim Fathers, bringing to a new world beliefs and institutions which, in their own country, had become impossible. They founded Hēmeroskopeion (the 'Watch-tower of the Morning', at Denia or Ifach), and other colonies along the east coast of Spain; and their colony at Marseilles founded a daughter city, Emporion (Ampurias), in northern Catalonia (535–520 B.C.). To this city the natives of the country came down from the hills to market their goods; and as the place increased in size they were given streets of their own, separated by a wall and shut off from the Greek quarter at night.

We may wonder how the Greek pilots ever managed to find Spain at all: they had neither the navigating instruments nor the geographical knowledge of Columbus or the Portuguese. For coastal sailing, their chief standby was a *periplus*, a sailing-book, giving every cape and harbour or other landmark useful for navigation. There is in existence a *periplus* of Spain made by a sailor from Marseilles before 530 B.C., and now preserved in a much later Latin poem by Avienus. It mentions the native tribes and towns of the coast, and tells us much of what Spain was like in the sixth century B.C. The course of the Phocaean sailors across the open sea, before they reached the coast, can be traced in another way: by a line of Phocaean place-names ending in *-oussa*. They sailed from island to island: Pithēkoussa (Ischia), Ichnoussa (Sardinia), Meloussa (Menorca?),

Kromyoussa (Majorca), Pityoussa (Ibiza), and so to
Hēmeroskopeion, whence they might coast along to
Kontinoussa (Cadiz) and finally to Ophioussa (Cabo
da Roca, at the mouth of the Tagus).

When they got there, what kind of country and
people did they find? The southern and eastern
coasts of Spain—which were all the Greeks knew—are
not unlike the coasts they knew all over the Mediterranean, in their own country, in Italy, and in Libya.
But the whole Spanish peninsula contains many types
of land and climate, from the olives and vineyards of
the Catalonian seaboard to the hot ricefields of the
lower Guadalquivir, and from the wet granite hills of
Galicia to the Valencian orange-groves or the palm-
trees of Elche, where it seldom rains. Between these
coasts lies the great stretch of the lion-coloured *meseta*
or table-land, crossed by bright green stripes along the
rivers. Some of these rivers have made broad basins
of deep soil. Wheat and fruit, as well as olives and
vines, will grow in the wide Guadalquivir valley, and
the middle Douro irrigates cornfields like the cornfields
of Lombardy. But the common idea of Spain as a
fertile, lazy land of summer is true only in very few
parts. Over most of the country life is difficult,
strenuous, and poor. Ploughs which would scarcely
dent the rich soil of England scratch the thin, stony
earth of Castile to grow barley; earth is carried up on
the backs of men, in baskets, to make a pocket for a
vine near Denia; water is brought for miles or pumped
laboriously by a donkey. The shepherds of Andalusia
and Estremadura drive their flocks 200 miles every
spring, and back again in autumn, to find summer
pastures. Even in rainy Galicia, cattle are fed through

the winter on gorse, beaten into a pulp with sticks by the farmer and his family. Over the inlands the climate swings between blazing, waterless heat and a long winter of bitter winds, with storms and floods of devastating violence. The land has bred people of different sorts, but nearly all of them stubborn; the sea has had less influence, except on the coast of Biscay, where a sailor race, the Basques, signed with Edward III of England the treaty which first established the principle of the freedom of the seas.

Besides differences of climate, Spain is everywhere cut up by mountains, and the mountains have tended to divide the people into small independent groups. This geographical condition of the land has been responsible for the most deeply rooted Spanish tradition, the tradition on which nearly all the other Spanish traditions depend: political separatism.

The first known inhabitants of Spain have been given the names of *Capsienses* and *Cantabro-Pyreneans*, the former having come originally from North Africa and the latter from the south of France. Spain possesses one of the most splendid memorials of primitive man to be found anywhere in the world: the rock-paintings in caves, and particularly those in the Cave of Altamira in the province of Santander.

By the time the Phocaeans came, however, Spain was dominated by two other races, Iberians and Celts. The Iberians, invading from North Africa, had taken possession of the richest portions of the peninsula: Andalusia, and the east coastal rim, along as far as the Rhône. These are the only parts that can be called Mediterranean in type; and the Iberians were a Mediterranean people, sophisticated, commercial, and artistic. The more warlike Iberians of the north-east were the ancestors of the Catalans; the Iberians of Valencia were the most gifted sculptors and vase-painters; the Tartessians of Andalusia were luxurious, clean, highly civilized, and strongly averse from fighting: *maxime imbelles*, Livy calls them. They had laws written in verse, and their chiefs, according to Polybius, lived in sumptuous palaces like those of the Phaeacian king in Homer, and ate off gold and silver plate. Their dancers were famous, and might, as the poet Martial said, have made even the austere Hippolytus lose his self-control.

Iberian artists learnt much from the Greeks, but they gave a Spanish twist to all their work. They liked to represent animals, flowers, and natural subjects, and already showed the abiding Spanish passion for bulls. The little bronze figures from the sanctuary of Cerro de los Santos, the strange stone beasts of the Murcian region, the delicate vase-paintings, and above all the magnificent bust of 'The Lady of Elche', all show how quick the Iberians were to feel Greek influence, and how sensitive they were to beautiful things.

The Celts, who invaded Spain in the seventh century B.C., made their lasting home in the west and north-west—an Atlantic type of country like Brittany or Cornwall. Strange tales were told to Strabo of these remote north-western regions, where the sun fell into the sea with a sizzle, logan-stones could be set rocking on the coast, the people performed moonlight dances, and were bestial in their habits and fierce to strangers. On the central plateau, inhabited by mixed Celtic and Iberian tribes, the Celts dominated the rest by their vigour and managing instincts. Some scholars believe

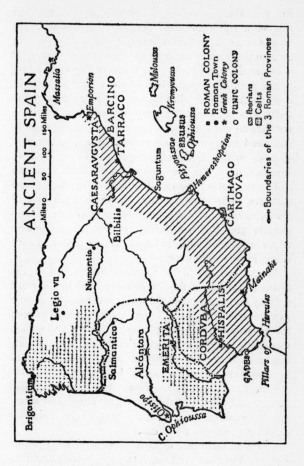

ANCIENT SPAIN

Miles 0 50 100 150 Miles

Massalia

Brigantium

Legio VII

Numantia

Bilbilis

CAESARAVGVSTA
Emporion
BARCINO
TARRACO

Saguntum

Pityousae
EBUSUS
Ophiussa

Hemeroskopeion

CARTHAGO
NOVA

Mainake

HISPALIS

CORDVBA

EMERITA

Alcántara

Salmantica

Obisipo
C. Ophioussa

GADES

Pillars of Hercules

Malousa

Kromyousa

■ ROMAN COLONY
● Roman Town
★ Greek Colony
○ PUNIC COLONY

▨ Iberians
⊞ Celts

●●● Boundaries of the 3 Roman Provinces

that they almost achieved the unity of Spain under the rule of a single people. 'Perhaps the Celts had a greater sense of political cohesion than the other peoples of Spain, a greater capacity for ruling over others, or even certain tendencies towards that wider view found in the political undertakings of the Castilian states in more recent times.' But the attempt failed, though the Celts were excellent fighters; it was usual for their warriors to swear to follow their chief unconditionally and uncritically, in the Germanic style, and not to survive his death. Some of the qualities for which both Iberians and Celts were noted in Strabo's time can still be recognized to-day: their hospitality, their grand manners, their arrogance, and above all, their love of freedom, which was shown in fierce resistance to conquerors and fanatical defence of beleaguered cities: Saguntum and Numantia begin the long list of famous sieges in Spanish history.

After the fall of Tyre, Carthage had picked up the Spanish markets of the Phoenicians, and in the third century B.C. the family of Hannibal began to pursue a new imperialist policy in Spain, to get money and men for a second war against Rome. The Carthaginian merchants lived on in the cities of the south, contributing much to the life of Spain, as Oriental or African peoples have so often done; but the Carthaginian armies were destroyed. When Hannibal's Spanish Empire crossed the Ebro, Rome intervened, and a new epoch began in which Spain was to be painfully subdued to Roman domination.

The long resistance of Spain produced many heroic figures: Viriathus the Lusitanian, whom Livy describes in terms that might have applied to the Mexican Pancho

Villa—a shepherd turned poacher and bandit, and at
last the leader of an army which kept Rome at bay all
over western Spain for eight years (147–139 B.C.); then
the Numantines, who broke two Roman armies before
Scipio starved them out (133), and whose example
(portrayed in Cervantes' monumental drama *The Siege
of Numancia*) helped to keep up the spirits of Madrid
in the long siege of 1936–39; and finally the anonymous
fighters of Galicia and Asturias who defied Agrippa in
their mountains (27–16 B.C.). These splendid enemies
fired the imagination even of Roman historians, and
tradition has exaggerated the cruelties and extortions
of the earlier Romans in Spain, without remembering
their later benefits.

The conquest had been forced on Rome, in the first
place, by military necessity, to secure Italy against
Carthage. Then came the knowledge of the silver of
Cartagena and the Pyrenees, the gold of Calatayud and
Río Tinto; and gradually all the Spanish metals and
mines were exploited. In many important Spanish
mines the traces of Roman workings are still visible;
sometimes the soil has been entirely removed, and the
course of rivers changed; in most places the veins of
precious metals have been exhausted. But when the
Romans had time to think of other things besides
soldiering and getting rich, they did much for the
Spanish people. It was two centuries before they had
conquered Spain, but a century after the conquest was
complete a Spaniard, Trajan, was chosen to be ruler
of the Roman Empire. Spaniards were filling high
military and civil offices, and the leading Latin writers
were Spanish as often as Italian. From a Spanish
point of view, this was a great period in the history of

the country, and one of the few periods in which the Spaniards have been politically happy and successful.

Spain has always had certain never-ending problems which different governments have faced in different ways: some well and some badly. The chief of these enduring problems is usually described as Spanish individualism. 'The proud Spaniard', it is often said by foreign observers, 'will never submit to this or that régime.' Strabo put this view more accurately when he said the Spaniards were 'bad mixers', or hard to unite. Many subsequent administrations have tried to cure this by over-centralization. Augustus, more wisely, cured it by granting an unusual degree of local autonomy, both in the larger divisions of Spain and in the towns. He had divided the peninsula into three provinces: Tarraconensis, Baetica (which is roughly Andalusia), and Lusitania (which, with some changes, has survived as Portugal). Within the provinces were smaller districts called *conventus*, which were elsewhere mere juridical divisions, but in Spain had some organization and sentiment of their own, like an English shire.

The Romans also had to adapt their central government to the strong local patriotism of the Spanish town or clan. The Iberians had a municipal system of their own, which fitted in very well with the Roman idea; for the Roman Empire, having grown up out of a city, still liked to work through a cell-system of provincial towns. Spain has always been a land of small towns with vigorous local feeling, as may be seen in Lope de Vega's great play *Fuente Ovejuna*—said to be the favourite play of the Russian army—in which the hero is the whole village. As late as 1924, in

Jimena de la Frontera in Andalusia, there was an un-official sovereign village council; and something similar has been reported from Mexico, where a legally elected municipal council existed as a shadow beside the traditional Council which had come down from primitive times. But at first the Iberian towns were not at all what a Roman meant by a town: they were little independent forts on hill-tops, pugnacious and poor. They had to be brought down on to richer and lower land, pacified, and finally made 'Latin' by being given a municipal charter. The failure of the Moslems, in later times, was largely due to their lack of municipal development; the success of the Romans was to take over the Iberian municipal tradition and recast it in a richer and more developed Latin form.

The Celts, on the other hand, had few or no towns. Strabo says they lived by stealing one another's sheep, and ate butter instead of olive oil. The reference to butter shows that they were not agricultural but pastoral. In the Roman view, agriculture was the first condition of a peaceful society, and towns a mark of higher civilization. Strabo, in a happy phrase, describes the Roman achievement among the Spanish Celts as 'making them not only peaceful, but some of them *political*'—i.e. bourgeois or town-dwelling. It would be difficult to find a better description of what Romanization in Spain meant. In particular, peace and local autonomy made the Spaniards able to com-bine, as they had never done before. A memorable example is the great Roman bridge over the Tagus—now known by its Arabic name of Alcántara—which was built by subscription among eleven small, undis-tinguished towns in Lusitania. Then there were the

B

great provincial Councils of elected Spanish representatives from the towns, meeting to discuss such
problems as military service, which affected them all.
Finally, Spain was bound together by a common
Roman law, and by the Latin language, which was
spoken by the richer Spaniards everywhere and by the
whole people in some parts, until the influence of the
Church made it universal.

Spain is full of great Roman monuments, some of
which were built by rich individual Spaniards—for
the principle of public service by rich local citizens
was fundamental in Greece and Rome as it is in the
United States of America, and the Spaniards quickly
caught the Roman habit. Other great works were
built in Roman colonies such as Emerita (Mérida)—a
magnificent city which shows the Roman passion
for civilizing unlikely places, regardless of their economic value as sites. Emerita had to have three
long aqueducts to make it habitable. Augustus in
Lusitania, like the builders of the Dnieperstroi dam
in Russia, thought first and foremost in terms of a
political and social mission, and then created the
economic conditions for its fulfilment. But modern
Portugal moved its backbone to the coast—to the rich
trading cities of Lisbon and Oporto—and Mérida sank
into insignificance.

How far, it may be asked, did Rome affect the minds
and ideas of ordinary people in Spain? The answer
is different in different parts of the country, for
Romanization, whatever else it was, was elastic. But
Rome attempted no deep intellectual conversion, and
did not want to make everybody speak and think like
Italians. For a true picture of life in the small places

of Roman Spain, we might turn to the Spanish poet, Martial, who came back to the primitive simplicity of his country home near Bilbilis (Calatayud) in Aragon, after a gay Bohemian life in Rome:

'Here we live lazily and work pleasantly in Boterdum and Platea—these are our rough Celtiberian place-names—and I enjoy a vast and shameless sleep. Often I don't wake up till after ten, and I'm making up all the sleep I've lost for thirty years. We know no such thing as a toga: if you want one, they give you the nearest rug off a broken chair. I get up to a glorious fire, heaped with logs from the oak-forest; and the land-agent's wife crowns it with her pots and pans. Then the beautiful young huntsman comes, and the land-agent doles out rations to the boys, and asks leave to have his long hair cut. This is how I love to live and die.'

There is also the other side to the picture: the letter Martial wrote on another day, saying that Bilbilis was a stupid little place, with no good conversation, no books, no theatres, and spite instead of literary taste. Yet that, too, corresponds with Strabo's modest description of Roman aims: to make people peaceful and bourgeois—while expecting them to live up to a Roman standard of public service. In that sense, the rough little towns which combined to build the great bridge of Alcántara were highly Romanized, and the people who ploughed the land outside the towns, instead of fighting one another, were Romanized too.

The elder Pliny, writing in the first century A.D., describes the country and its men in words which we should scarcely alter to-day: 'Next to Italy I myself should rank the coastal regions of Spain. Some parts of Spain are wretchedly poor; but where the land does yield, it is fertile in wheat, oil, wine, horses, and all kinds of metals. As far as that goes, it is equalled by Gaul, but in its barren places Spain wins, with its esparto, its mica, the lovely colours of its dyes, the ardour of its workmen, the skill of its slaves, the bodily endurance of its people, and their vehement spirit.'

The outstanding men of Spain were naturally more Roman in their culture and ideas than the ordinary people: yet they, too, sometimes show qualities which can be recognized in the Spaniards of later history. Besides emperors, generals, and civil servants, Roman Spain produced writers and thinkers. Martial's satirical humour and delight in country people reappear in later Spanish literature. A different school of writing flourished in Córdoba, a brilliant city in Roman times, as it was under the Moslems, and famous for its poetry and its olive oil. Cicero said the poetry sounded as if it had got mixed with the oil; and much Spanish verse has been written in the staccato, clashing, declamatory vein of Lucan, parodied by Petronius in his *Satyricon*. Lucan is Spanish, too, in his passionate political feeling, his hatred of tyranny and of emperor-worship, which brought him an early death at the hands of Nero.

The younger Seneca, who also came from Córdoba, was a Stoic teacher of the best type, with clearly defined methods of physical, intellectual, and moral education. Reason, he held, was the infallible light which guided man on his path, and distinguished not only between truth and error but also between right and wrong. Virtue was not a gift: it was the result of an effort of will. Moral education, therefore, was not the teaching of duties but the training of the will. The basis of education was the curiosity of the child, but the process of learning went on as long as life lasted, though it was essential to make full use of time and not postpone work until to-morrow. 'Would anyone believe that this was said by a Spaniard?' a modern Spanish educator has asked. But there was something curiously Spanish in Seneca's famous and rather theatrical suicide, at the command of his least creditable pupil, Nero.

Quintilian was a man of another mould. He came from the valley of the Ebro, 'a country of sobriety, obstinacy, and common sense' He was a teacher at Rome, and Vespasian endowed him with a chair of rhetoric out of public funds. Quintilian had to give rules for the training of public speakers, and in doing so he composed the first text-book of education: 'a practical guide, free from abstruse philosophical and psychological theories, revealing a shrewd teacher seriously at work.'

After the introduction of Christianity, Spain began to feel some separate national consciousness, apart from the Roman Empire. There have been no more typical Spaniards than Hosius, Bishop of Córdoba, writing firmly to forbid an Emperor to meddle in matters concerning the Church [1]; Prudentius the poet, author of 'truculent hymns of martyrdom' in lyric verse of exquisite colour and beauty; Priscillian the heretic, who admitted dancing into the services of the Church (a custom still observed in the 'Dance of the Seises' before the High Altar at Seville); and Orosius, who wrote with violence and bitterness against Rome when the Roman world was falling to pieces, and Spain was already feeling the helpless dread of the invasions of the barbarians.

[1] μὴ τίθει σεαυτὸν εἰς τὰ ἐκκλησιαστικά.

CHAPTER II
THE MOSLEM PROVINCES

THERE had been two main types, so far, of colonization in Spain: the Greek, radiating from a few disconnected cities on the coast, and the Roman, controlling the whole country but encouraging local self-management through the municipal spirit of country towns. The third type, the Moslem, was very different. It was a community of believers, all equal before the law, with a leader who was in theory a shepherd but in practice a despot. They were brethren, but proudly independent; they had municipal officers, but no municipal spirit.

The Moslem community had a basis which was ethical and religious: a man's duty was not to the community but to his faith. Mutual help to a brother Moslem was a legal obligation, a religious duty; but it was help given by one independent individual to his equal. There was, of course, a principle of unity in their society; but that principle which in other societies is called *polis*, *civitas*, State, in Islam is personified by Allah, 'the Supreme power acting in the common interest'. The Moslem system had qualities likely to appeal to the Spanish mind, more than the formalism inherited from Rome, or the Germanic conceptions introduced by the Visigoths; and Moslems in Spain believed that all men were equal before the law at a time when that was practically unknown in the rest of Europe. On the debit side, however, must be set the tendency to anarchy of a people whose spiritual home or background was the desert; and their consequent incapacity for organization and discipline accentuated failings which had always been latent in the people of Spain.

The Moslem colonists of Spain are often spoken of as Moors, because on the first occasion, and on other occasions also, they came from Morocco. But their leaders were usually Arabs; and the Arabs were no Pilgrim Fathers fleeing from religious persecution to found an ideal republic in a new world. They were more like conquistadores, urged on (as the Spaniards were later in America) by a triumphant, proselytizing faith: a chosen people to whom had been entrusted the furtherance of good and the suppression of evil.

The Arabs had entered on their career of expansion soon after the *Hégira*, the Flight of the Prophet with a few chosen companions from Mecca to Medina, which took place in the year 622. The leaders of the Moslem expansion in Spain were also Arabs, but the colonists themselves were often men who belonged to Berber tribes in Morocco. Tāriq, who led the first expedition and defeated Roderick the last Visigothic king of Spain, was a Berber. The men he brought with him are said, according to the most moderate estimate, to have consisted of 300 Arabs and Syrians and 7000 Berbers, while further reinforcements sent across the Straits before the decisive battle amounted to some 12,000 Berbers. The Commander-in-Chief (who took charge after Tāriq had won the battle and proved that colonization might be attempted) was Mūsā Ibn Nusair, an Arab belonging to a tribe from the Yemen in South Arabia.

Tāriq and Mūsā are still remembered among the Moslem peoples of to-day as the conquerors of Spain—

the men by whom (as the Arabic historians say) Spain was 'opened up': for the word is used in Arabic in the sense of conquest, just as it is by European writers when they mean an act of wanton aggression. Tāriq is immortalized in the name of Gibraltar, a corruption of *Jabal Tāriq*, the mountain of Tāriq; while Mūsā, too, has a mountain named after him: Jabal Mūsā on the coast of Morocco, one of the Pillars of Hercules. Mūsā had a fleet of small ships, in which his men were ferried across from Tangier to Spain. His sailors were mainly Copts: Christians from Egypt whose form of worship resembled that of the modern Abyssinians, but whose descent can be traced back to the ancient Egyptians. It is important to bear these different peoples in mind—these Arabs, Syrians, Berbers, and Copts—because many of them eventually settled in Spain. They have been called indifferently 'Moors'; but actually they came from very different places, and reacted in very different ways, in their new country in the West.

The Arabs were leaders, picked men from different parts of Arabia; men who (as it turned out) brought all their family feuds with them, so that all the quarrels of Arabia were fought out in Spain. To wars of rival Moslem sects were added local jealousies as well: Yemenite Arabs from South Arabia could never put up with Qaisites from the North; in Spain, they could not settle in the same districts without quarrelling. They fraternized, however, with the Spanish Christians; and as time went on, the most prosperous parts of Moslem Spain are said to have been those in which descendants of Yemenite Arabs and Visigothic or Roman Spanish Christians lived side by side. But the majority of the Moslem colonists were Berbers; men from what is now known as the Riff, the mountainous country just across the Straits of Gibraltar, and other parts of Morocco, including the Great and Little Atlas Mountains and the desert beyond. They were the strength and the weakness of Moslem colonization in Spain: it was they who first made it possible, and they who ultimately destroyed it by their fanaticism.

Modern research has discredited the legendary account of the cause of the conquest. It used to be said that the invasion was a consequence of the dishonour of Count Julian's daughter: Roderick, king of the Visigoths, saw her bathing in the Tagus at Toledo (she must have been a strong swimmer, to bathe there) and made her his mistress, whence Julian's revenge and his treachery in bringing men from Morocco to overthrow Roderick and intervene in a domestic quarrel. Roderick was certainly the last Visigothic king; he had usurped the throne of Witiza; while Julian may have been in the service of Byzantium: Exarch of Ceuta under the Emperor Constantine IV.

Roderick was at Pamplona, at the other end of Spain, when Tāriq landed, as Harold was in the north when William the Conqueror landed at Pevensey. He hurried down with every available man; but he was unwise enough to hand over his army to Sisibert, who belonged to the faction of Witiza. The battle of Guadalete took place near Cape Trafalgar, in a wide plain adjoining the Laguna de la Janda which can still be seen, half drained, as one looks down from the main road from Algeciras to Cadiz. The battle lasted for two days. Roderick was betrayed by Sisibert, by 'Uncle Oppas' (as Gibbon calls him), archbishop of Seville, and by all the partisans of Witiza. Roderick either died fighting, or was eaten by wild beasts in the mountains, or (as the ballads say) was nibbled in a tender place by a serpent as he lay in his tomb for a penance.

Tāriq did not stop to inquire what had happened to Roderick: he made straight for Roderick's capital, Toledo. A small force was left to besiege Córdoba, with the help of those Visigoths who had been partisans of the late King Witiza and who were therefore hostile to Roderick. Only gradually did this 'fifth column' realize that the troops, invited from Africa to help in the settlement of a domestic disagreement, had come to stay as permanent colonists.

It is interesting to consider the attitude of these men, Arabs and Syrians and Copts and Berbers, who had come to Spain for the first time. What did they think of it? As time went on, it dawned on the most thoughtful men in the Moslem army that here was a country in which many things had happened before their own history had begun, before the Prophet of Allah had come into the world with his message. Berbers like Tāriq had probably heard of the Romans; some Berber tribes had even been Christian; Fathers of the Church like Tertullian and St. Augustine of Hippo were of Berber stock. But Arabs like Mūsā were in a very different position. Less than a hundred years before, the whole world—as they knew it—had been in what they termed the Age of Ignorance: that is, before the Coran had been revealed. Since then, since the Flight to Medina and the triumph of the Prophet, the Arabs had come across many peoples, many ways of living and of building houses to live in; many religions and many attitudes to life. They had met with the civilization of Greece under various forms: Syrian, Byzantine, Graeco-Roman; but now for the first time—and above all at Mérida—the Moslem invaders of Spain found themselves face to face with the thoroughgoing civilization of an old Roman province.

Abū Ghālib, a native of Córdoba, in a book called *The Contentment of the Soul in the Contemplation of the Ancient Remains of Spain*,[1] says that the country was filled with the remains of buildings, temples and aqueducts and other wonderful constructions of the ancient kings of al-Andalus—by which the Moslems meant the Roman rulers of Spain. Between Lisbon and Talavera, 'on the river that comes from Toledo' (i.e. the Tagus), was the famous bridge known as Alcántara, *al-Qantarat as-saïf*, the Bridge of the Sword: one of the wonders of the world. It was very high—he gives measurements, and they are not far out—and on the top was a tower (the triumphal arch of the Alcántara bridge) with a brazen sword fixed in it. Whoever seized the handle and pulled might draw the sword about three spans; but no human strength had yet succeeded in drawing it further. The Middle Ages were already gathering about the noble Roman monument. Then there was the tower and idol of Cadiz (the Roman lighthouse), which had not its equal in the world except for another of the same size and shape which stood on a high promontory in Galicia. The idol was said to hold in its right hand a bunch of keys.

[1] Quoted by Al-Maqqarī in *The Breath of Fragrance from the Fresh Branch of al-Andalus* (Chapter III).

The belief prevailed all over al-Andalus that underneath the idol an immense treasure was buried; but when later, in 1145–46, one of the Berber rulers caused the tower and idol to be pulled down, and search made for the treasure, nothing was to be found.

The geographer al-Bakrī mentions the ruins of buildings erected by the Romans and 'the talismans constructed by their philosophers'. He included in these the towers of Cadiz and Galicia, the amphitheatre at Saguntum, the Bridge of the Sword, the aqueduct at Tarragona, 'and many other stupendous buildings scattered over the country and for the most part attributed to one of the ancient Kings of al-Andalus whose name was Hercules'. Another notable aqueduct was that which conveyed fresh water from a spring in 'the district of idols' (the site of a temple?) near Jerez, to the island of Cadiz, crossing an arm of the ocean on a long line of arches. The vestiges of the ancient kings of al-Andalus included the causeways (Roman roads) which traversed it in all its length; and Moslems were astonished that these roads were, by the orders of Caesar, provided with milestones on which his name was carved as well as that of the city to which the road led and the distance from Rome.

The most obvious things in Spain, then, when the Arabs and Berbers reached it, were Roman. The invaders marched along the Roman roads and crossed the Roman bridges; they saw Roman walls, Roman theatres, Roman temples. Such things existed, to some extent, in other countries which were once Roman and became Moslem : in Syria, for instance, and in North Africa; but in Spain there were Roman remains everywhere.

Into this land of Roman roads and waterworks there
had burst in the fifth century (A.D. 409) various tribes
of barbarians, who proceeded to sack and destroy, and
then in some cases to settle: Suevi, Vandals, Alani,
Visigoths.   They came from the East: the Suevi from
somewhere between the Rhine and the Danube; the
Vandals, from between the Oder and the Vistula; the
Alani, from between the Sea of Azov and the Caucasus.
The Visigoths had originally been an army in the
service of the Romans.   Yet by the time the Moslems
arrived there was nothing to show that any of the
barbarians had ever existed, except the Visigoths.
These had, it is true, a certain degree of civilization,
with possibilities which looked forward into the future.
They had their own laws—Teutonic laws and customs
—and their own art.   There is the crown of one of the
Visigothic kings: a fantastically beautiful golden crown,
different from any crown that any other people has
ever seen or thought of : Roger Fry called it 'an
incomparable piece of jewelry '.   There are also in
existence several Visigothic churches; and they have
an interest in the history of Spanish architecture
comparable with that of Saxon churches in the architectural history of England.

When Mūsā's men reached Córdoba, the first thing
they saw was a large Visigothic church—St. Vincent's
—a curious mixture of late Roman and Byzantine
styles, built on the site of a temple of Janus, near the
Roman bridge where the Roman road (Via Augusta)
crossed the river Baetis, now called by its Arabic
name Guadalquivir, the Great River.   The Moslems
did not attack the church, or plunder it, or burn it,
or pull it down.   They bought it—half of it: and

while the Christians were allowed to keep one end for
church services, the Moslems used the other end as a
mosque, and they went on sharing it with the Christians
for the space of forty years. After all, the Christians
had a Holy Book, just as the Moslems had themselves; and Moslem law justified them in making
this kind of distinction between unbelievers who had
a Holy Book and those who had not. Then in 785,
'Abd-ar-Rahmān I, the first 'Emir descended from
the caliphs', bought the other half of the church of
St. Vincent from the Christians, and built part of the
mosque which is in Córdoba to-day.

'Abd ar-Rahmān I was a Syrian by birth. It was he
who planted the first palm-tree in Spain to remind
him of his native land; and he wished the new mosque
at Córdoba to remind him of the Grand Mosque in his
old home, Damascus. The new building he planned
was a low-roofed hall, with numerous rows of columns
leading up to the wall on the side nearest Mecca, to
which all Moslems turn when they say their prayers.
In the middle of this wall was the prayer-niche. In
front of the mosque was an open court with fountains
in the middle, at which the faithful performed their
ablutions; and there was a tower, a minaret, from
which they were called to prayer. Outside, the walls
were kept as plain as possible; inside, the intention
was to produce the effect of a forest of columns. The
eyes of the faithful were not to be raised to heaven by
majestic heights, domes, or 'a spire to point to God';
they were to look straight in the direction of Mecca
and fix their minds on the Prophet. Originally there
were as many entrances as there were rows of columns:
one between each two rows; while out in the courtyard

the rows of columns were continued by rows of orange-trees.

'Abd ar-Rahmān I afterwards bought the other half of the cathedral, and in 785 he began the building which is there to-day. His successors added to it. One can see how each new Emir, each 'Abd ar-Rahmān or Hakam or Hishām, left his mark on it. At first it had eleven aisles, separated by rows of columns. 'Abd ar-Rahmān II (822–852) kept the number of aisles the same, but lengthened them on the side towards the river. 'Abd ar-Rahmān III, the first Caliph (912–961), built a new minaret; Hakam II (961–976) built out further in the direction of the river. Al-Mansūr, grand vizier to the ineffectual caliph Hishām II, added eight more aisles and enlarged the Court of Orange Trees.

The Great Mosque of Córdoba is an index to the different rulers of Moslem Spain. It is still one of the most striking and most beautiful things in the Spanish world, and nothing makes a greater impression on the mind than the interior. It seems dark, at first: a mysterious forest of columns, with heavy overarching boughs. Then gradually, as the modern traveller wanders through it, he begins to notice something in the middle; something which spoils the perspectives between the columns, and is eventually discerned as the shape of a large, Christian church. It is no use blaming the people who built their church in the middle of the mosque. Charles V was right when he told the cathedral chapter that they had built something which they could have built anywhere, and spoilt something which they could find nowhere else in the world; but, after all, the church had been there first—

the Visigothic church of St. Vincent which the Moslems had found when they first crossed the Roman bridge. The fact that a new (sixteenth-century) church was built inside the mosque has probably been responsible for its preservation.

From 1236, when Córdoba was captured by the Christians, the mosque was used as a cathedral, practically as it stood, for 300 years. All the conquerors did was to 'purify' the place, which they accomplished by blocking up the open ends of the aisles leading out into the Court of Orange Trees, and shutting out air and light. The idea of the Moslems had been that the invisible presence of Allah should be felt, both inside and out. The regular description of a desert, or an empty space, in Arabic literature (in *The Thousand and One Nights*, and elsewhere) is: 'Nothing there but the presence of Allah'. Those long lines of columns in the darkness of the mosque were intended to be a continuation of the long lines of orange-trees in the courtyard outside. The Christian conquerors did not understand that. They shut up the ends of all the aisles except the one opposite the prayer-niche, and that opening became the principal door. The ends of the other aisles, now blocked up, were made into little chapels, where devout women say their prayers and minor canons keep their vestments. Once the ends of the columned aisles had been blocked up, the lines of orange-trees had no meaning. They had completely lost their function, which was to lead gradually from the world without to the world within. That was the poetry of the Moslem conception of the relation between the outer world and the inner, between body and spirit; and the Christians, in their scorn for Islam and all who professed Islam, did not have the sense to use a poetical conception and an architectural conception, the relation between a building and a garden, which would have suited Christian theology as well as it suited the theology of Islam. But that was not all. The fountains were allowed to get out of order. Among Moslem Spaniards, washing had been compulsory: the somewhat formal ablution in the Court of Orange Trees was only the prelude to a visit to one of the three hundred public baths which there were in the city of Córdoba. The Christian Spaniards dispensed with all that. Christians, so the Moslems thought, never washed at all. They were sprinkled with water at the time they were born, and thus relieved from the obligation of washing for the rest of their lives. That, perhaps, is not an orthodox view of Christian baptism; but it was a view held in Moslem Spain.

The Moslems in Spain eventually became just as Spanish as the Christians were. There were Spanish Moslems and Spanish Christians; but they were all Spaniards, and what they did and thought belongs equally to the Spanish world. Spain does not mean only Christian Spain.

The mixed origins of the Moslem invaders have already been pointed out. It is interesting to see what the population of Spain was like after colonization had gone on for three or four generations. At the time of the conquest large numbers of Spanish and Visigothic Christians were converted to Islam. The alternatives were not conversion or death, but Islam with equality before the law, or Christianity with inequality and income tax. Those who remained Christians had to pay for the privilege, and there were some who were willing to pay. There was also a good deal of intermarriage between Moslems and Christians. The Moslem colonists brought no women with them, and they all followed the example of the son of Mūsā, marrying into Spanish and Visigothic families; so that throughout the country the mothers of the next generation of Moslems were all Spanish.

Modern Spanish orientalists have studied the records of the slave-market at Córdoba at various periods. Buying a slave was not so simple a matter as might be thought. It had to be done in the presence of a notary, and the purchaser had to state what he wanted the slave for, and how he proposed to look after her. The greatest demand was for fair-skinned slaves from the North, usually described in the documents as Galicians. The result was that although, according to Arab custom, the children were given the names of their ancestors in the male line only (So-and-so the son of So-and-so the son of So-and-so) and thus inherited an imposing array of Arab names, the purity of their Arab descent was diminished, by crossing with Spanish strains, in every successive generation; and it was remarked—it was a well-worn joke in Moslem Spain—that the more Arab names a man had, the less Arab blood he had in his veins. It is also wrong to assume that most Christians fled to the North at the time of the conquest; and it is absurd to think of the Christian reconquest as a war lasting eight centuries between Latins and Goths in the North and Andalusian Arabs in the South. What happened was that, in the Moslem parts of Spain, a mixture of races took place, and that very rapidly.

From the third and fourth generation, after the Moslem colonization had begun, many Spanish Moslems were bilingual. Those who were of Arab descent often spoke two languages, and those who were of purely Christian Spanish origin often spoke two languages also. Besides Arabic, which was the official language, a Romance *patois* was spoken; and this *patois* (the beginning of modern Spanish) was used particularly by the Christians who lived, like the majority of Spanish Christians after the conquest, under Moslem rule. They were called *Mozárabes*, i.e. 'arabized' or 'would-be Arabs'.[1] There were, in fact, four languages in use in Moslem Spain: (1) Classical Arabic, the language of religion and of men of letters; (2) Colloquial Arabic, the language of administration and government; (3) Ecclesiastical Latin, a purely ritual language, used only by Mozarabic Christians; and (4) a Romance dialect, mainly derived from Low Latin, and one day to become one of the great literary and administrative languages of the world: *Romance castellano* or Spanish.

The official history of Spain under the Emirs of Córdoba is full of revolts; but official history inevitably exaggerates their importance. Life went on; and the time was on the whole—when compared with that of the rest of Europe—a time of well-being and progress. Spain under the first Emirs appointed by Damascus had been a colony; under the Emirs descended from the caliphs it became a prosperous independent state,

[1] From an Arabic participle, *musta'rib*, not, as some scholars have supposed, from the Latin *mixti arabes*.

although the Moslem dominions in Spain were not really united until the time of 'Abd ar-Rahmān III, who had himself proclaimed caliph in 929. The Arabs, and to a less extent the Berbers also, had one of the greatest opportunities in their history of achieving civilization, and their culture was something that really deserved the name, for it was the culture of men who cultivated not only their minds but also their gardens.

These Arabic-speaking Spaniards have left a permanent mark on Spain and on all Spanish-speaking countries all over the world. Names of places, hundreds of them, in Spain and in Spanish America, are Arabic or partly derived from Arabic. Some of the commonest objects of everyday Spanish life still have Arabic names, while many of the modern Spanish words connected with building, tiles, carpets, flowers, fruit, gardens, agriculture, and above all irrigation— watering the garden—are Arabic words, taken over into Spanish as they stood, so that these things have much the same names to-day in Spain and Morocco.

The Moslems in Spain taught people that water was a thing which had to be looked after carefully and made the most of. Irrigation, they found, had to be elaborately regulated, particularly in the Vega round Granada, and in Murcia, and above all in Valencia. In Valencia there is still a Water Court which sits twice a week to try cases of abuse of water. The Court can sentence an offender to have his water cut off; and in the dry gardens of Valencia, it is as fatal to say 'Off with his water' as it would be to say 'Off with his head'. It is a people's tribunal, and no records are kept; but the technical terms in use come mainly from the time of the Moslems.

As far as Córdoba was concerned, this agreeable and satisfactory form of civilization received a deadly blow at the beginning of the eleventh century. The responsibility must fall mainly on the grand vizier, Al-Mansūr. Al-Mansūr had sent an army every year to the uttermost parts of Spain; but instead of trying to colonize, or civilize, the fierce Christians in their remote mountain states, 'opening up' (as the historians would have said) the whole of northern Spain and making it into a united Spanish state, he preferred to make it a desert, and to indulge in such feats as carrying off the bells from the cathedral of Santiago. At length Al-Mansūr died, and, as a monkish chronicler put it, was buried in hell. Hell at any rate came to Córdoba not long after he was gone.

In 1010 the city was captured and looted by Christians, and the place which Ferdinand the Saint, king of Castile, captured more than two centuries later was not the capital of a flourishing, civilized state, but a decayed provincial town. The intellectual leadership of Moslem Spain passed from Córdoba to Seville.

The fall of Córdoba was by no means the end of Moslem civilization in Spain; indeed the two hundred years which followed were among the most brilliant in Moslem Spanish history, in spite of the sudden and disconcerting political changes. The first period is that of the City States. These 'party kings', or *reyes de taifas*, as Spanish historians call them, were at first, in theory at any rate, officers of the last caliph, Hishām III, who had disappeared and was never heard of again.

The rulers of Seville who rose to power on the fall

of the caliphate of Córdoba came of Yemenite, South Arabian, stock. The family name was Ibn 'Abbād; Spanish writers spell it Benabet. The most famous of these kings was the last, Mu'tamid (1068–91), a man who was personally acquainted with the Cid and, as it happened, altered the whole course of the Cid's life. Spanish chroniclers spell his name Almutamiz. He was himself a considerable poet, and his life has the elements of poetic tragedy. The last king of Seville was faced by a difficult choice: he was not strong enough to stand alone, and for allies he had to decide between Castilians and Berbers—between Alfonso VI of Castile and León, and the Empire of the Berber puritans in the South of Morocco. He was certainly more attracted by the Castilians than by the Berbers, and he had given one of his daughters in marriage to Alfonso VI. But the Moslem holy men in Seville pressed for an alliance with their fellow-Moslems; and the Castilians were loth to admit that the king of Seville's daughter had ever been married to the king of Castile in any legal form. Al-Mu'tamid, therefore, was obliged to invite to Spain the puritan founder of the Marabout (Almorávid) dynasty, Yūsuf Ibn Tashfīn. Yūsuf accepted. He promised to intervene with a few 'volunteers', but came to Spain with a horde of black puritans from the Sahara, who destroyed the military forces of Alfonso VI utterly, in 1087. Then, having crushed the Christians, they proceeded to subdue the Spanish Moslems as well. They deprived Mu'tamid of his capital, Seville, and sent him in chains to Morocco. He had been a good king and a capable ruler. Even the Castilians were sorry for him, and he was celebrated by poets and story-tellers. The Berber regiments proved stronger, and he went down before a horde of religious fanatics.

But the fanaticism was short-lived, and the age of the two Berber dynasties—Almorávides (marabouts) and Almohades (unitarians)—is also that of the highest development in Spain of Moslem and Jewish thought; indeed it represents one of the furthest flights of the Spanish spirit at any period. The leaders of both Berber invasions were idealists, and the Almohade leader was a theologian and something of a philosopher as well. Ibn Tumart and his Almohade followers asserted not only the unity of God, but the complete spiritualization of the whole conception of God. They saw no reason in anthropomorphism, in the idea of God possessing a material body. The Almohade creed showed signs of a philosophic breadth of view lacking in most of its contemporaries and perhaps tending to pantheism. The arrival in Spain of Africans professing such ideas was generally regarded with horror; yet the Almohade period, barely a century in duration, produced the most profound and fertile Moslem Spanish thought. That it was fertile in Christendom also is shown immediately by the names of its chief exponents, universally known in their Latin forms.

The first of importance under the new régime was Avempace (Ibn Bājjā) of Saragossa. His chief problem was one which is as urgent to-day as it was then: how can the thinker, scholar, or man of science be free to live and work and express himself in a world controlled by the ignorant and fanatical? Avempace held that 'the greatest joy and the closest truth' were to be found in thought, and not (as with many other Spaniards, both Moslem and Christian) in the sensuous ecstasies of the mystic. The highest thing in a man's being was his intellect; but that intellect was only likely to be good if it joined itself to the one Active Intellect, which, in Avempace's view, belonged to God, and in fact was God. This position is the foundation of a view which afterwards went all over Europe under the name of Averroës. Avempace declared that in order to attain the ideal one must live rationally, which, in his time, was as much as to say in solitude; but he was regarded by orthodox Moslems as a heretic, and only the friendship of the Almorávid chiefs saved him. The Almohade rulers were more tolerant. There was no objection to the study of philosophy by the educated; the problem was, how much philosophy (or anything else) might be taught to the great mass of the people. The solution was drastic, though it compared favourably with that afterwards adopted in Christian Spain. The Almohade rulers decided that the majority should be taught nothing beyond the literal meaning of the Coran, with its strange metaphors and startling anthropomorphic imagery, like that of the Old Testament. The more instructed, however, were given to understand that there was no real difference between philosophy and theology—or, as we might say now, between science and religion—since both were phases of the same truth. Philosophers, they said—scientists, thinkers—should be free to go their own way, provided (and the proviso was important) that their speculations did not spread beyond their own circle.

An example of a Spanish thinker who was able, by accepting this proviso, to live 'a calm, contemplative life, secluded in princely libraries', was Ibn Tufail, a

Moslem whose writings have been translated into most modern European languages. Ibn Tufail had little hope that the great majority could ever be taught the truth. An emotional religion was needed 'to restrain the wild beast in man', and the masses should be left to the guidance of that religion. For the philosopher to try to teach the people better was rash; it was exposing himself to peril and his audience to the loss of what little spiritual comfort they had.

As regards their own lives two courses were open to the philosophers: they could devote themselves to study, with or without 'spiritual exercises', or they could boldly enter public life. Avempace and Ibn Tufail chose the former; but the greatest Moslem thinker of the time, Averroës, chose the latter.

Averroës was, like Avempace and Ibn Tufail, a Spaniard; he was born at Córdoba in 1126. He is said to have known Aristotle better than any of his contemporaries; but he knew him only in Arabic, and it is extraordinary that a man with a mind like his should never have thought it worth while to learn Greek to see what Aristotle had really said. The result was that Averroës knew an Aristotle streaked with neoplatonism, and some of the Arabic books that went under Aristotle's name were apocryphal. Averroës was no mystic, nor did he believe in solitary meditation. He liked to go about in public places and have contact with other people, though he always remained very much the philosopher. Philosophers, in his view, belonged to a class apart and there were many things which they should keep to themselves. That was also the view of the Almohade government, and life and freedom would have been impossible for

Averroës if he had not kept to that rule. Philosophy, he taught, agreed with religion, and religion recommended philosophy. Religion was true because it was revelation from God: and philosophy was true because it depended on the thought of the human mind. These truths could not contradict each other. There were two sides to revealed religion: meaning and interpretation. Only the literal meaning concerned the multitude; while the interpretation was a question for scholars, capable of philosophical reasoning, who must be allowed complete liberty in their opinions. They were not to communicate their interpretations to the people in general: the plain man's faith must be protected from all contact with philosophers who might unsettle him; but if the philosopher decided that the meaning of a passage was not literal, but allegorical, he was allowed complete liberty to say so to his pupils. Averroës would never have accepted the state of affairs in Christian Spain, where a Church could decide, and enforce, what might be interpreted and what might not. Like the more uncompromising Avempace, he was still concerned with the freedom of thought and expression.

In Moslem Spain, however, it was not the talkative Averroës who triumphed but the contemplative Ibn Tufail; and the most erotic of Spanish mystics, Ibn 'Arabī of Murcia, followed soon after. He is chiefly remembered to-day for his description of a journey into hell which contains many curious anticipations of Dante's Inferno.

The period of the Berber dynasties in Spain is remarkable, too, for the great development of Hispano-Jewish thought; and if it had not been for the help of

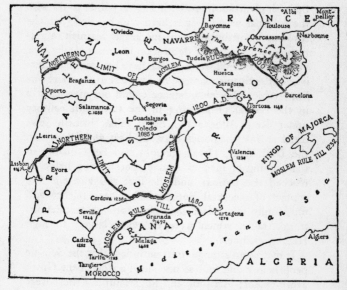

ISLAM IN SPAIN AND PORTUGAL

(from *The Legacy of Israel*)

the Jews, as intermediaries or translators, the Moslem contribution might never have become known in the rest of Europe.

The characteristic of the Jewish contribution to Spanish civilization is that it has very little to do with the external world. It is hardly to be seen (like the Moslem contribution) in medieval Spanish architecture, woodwork, or decoration in coloured tiles, nor yet in the Oriental words which have become characteristic of the Spanish language: for these are not Hebrew but Arabic. Jewish influence comes out most clearly in the revival of learning in the thirteenth century under King Alfonso the Sage. The Spanish Jews acted as intermediaries between East and West. In the Dark Ages, Greek thought had been mainly in the keeping of men of Arabic speech, long before it reached the Latins; and the first real and effective contact of medieval Europe with Greek science and philosophy took place in Spain, through translations from Arabic, which were conveyed largely through Hebrew channels.

It may seem strange to us nowadays that the Semitic peoples in Spain took so one-sided a view of the Greek achievement; Aristotle and the scientific writers were the only part of Greek civilization which they were able to appreciate. They had no occasion for Greek art: the God in whom they believed was invisible, and it was unthinkable that any man's hand could represent Him, or, indeed, any of His creatures. The Moslems, again, seem never to have known the tragedians or poets. Arabic poetry was something very different: it took centuries—even in Spain—to shake off the conventions of the desert; and Greek tragedy, with its perpetual conflict between man and gods, would have been inconceivable to the mind which accepted the religion of Islam, with its complete ascendancy of God over man. The Spanish Arabic historians might well have profited from the study of Herodotus—in arranging, for instance, the mass of historical material in *The Breath of Fragrance from the Fresh Branch of al-Andalus*; while the Sinbad-like stories in the *Odyssey* could hardly have failed to hold the attention of a people whose 'frame-stories', constructed on the principle of *Kalīla and Dimna* and *The Thousand and One Nights*, gave the first impulse to narrative prose in the Spanish language. But Greek science and philosophy were studied with avidity; they became Moslem subjects, far more living in their new Arabic dress than in the monkish Latin in which they returned to Europe, where they held the field until the revival of Greek studies at the Renascence.

The event which opened up communication between the scholars of Moslem Spain and those of England and France was the capture of Toledo by Alfonso VI, in 1085. Toledo, with its extraordinary mixed population of Moslems, Jews, Mozarabic Spanish Christians, immigrants from Castile and León, and ecclesiastics from France, became in the next two centuries a school of translation from Arabic into Latin. The wandering scholar from Oxford, Paris, or Salamanca would need, on arrival at Toledo, the help of some learned and accommodating Jewish savant, who would know where to find an Arabic manuscript of Aristotle, or one of the medical or musical writers of antiquity, which the foreign scholar was seeking. Having arranged to borrow it, the wandering scholar and the Jewish interpreter would sit down for many months in an attic, while the one would laboriously turn the Arabic into Latin, and the other laboriously take it down. Considering the difficulty of both languages, their utter dissimilarity, the fact that many turns of Arabic thought are as dependent on the structure of the language as are many of the concepts of German philosophy; considering also the fact that the works had not as a rule been thought in the first instance in Arabic at all, but in Greek, the difficulty of the problem may be imagined and the resulting confusion pardoned. Some of the translations brought back by the wandering scholars were read and understood, and had important effects on medieval learning; in others (in some of the early English treatises on music, for instance), one feels that both the wandering scholar and his Jewish interpreter sometimes lost the thread of what the Arabic author was saying; and what with the cramp and discomfort of the attic, the cold of Toledo in winter and the heat in summer, they have merely put down approximate Latin equivalents for the Arabic words in the Arabic order, and sometimes transliterated an Arabic technical term bodily into the text, because they had no idea what it meant. With all these difficulties, with the absence of grammars (except those in Arabic) and of dictionaries (except the few rough glossaries that were then to be had), it is wonderful that any translation was effected at all, and that the scholars' rough-and-ready Latin versions of Arabic translations of Aristotle were not further from the original Greek, and more heretical, than they actually were.

The Jewish thinkers also brought into Moslem Spanish thought complications which had not been there before. Ben Gabirol for instance (known to the Latins as Avicebron) introduced neoplatonic thought to the schools of the Peninsula (1012–58). Rabbi Ben Ezra (1092–1167), a Spanish Jew who travelled as far as London, taught that material events are inevitable, though the soul is free. But the most important Jewish philosopher in Spain was Moses Ben Maimūn, known to the Christian world as Maimonides (1135–1204). Like Averroës, he was born at Córdoba; but when he was thirteen Córdoba was captured by the Almohades, and Maimonides became a wandering Jew in Spain, Morocco, and Palestine, before he eventually settled in Cairo. He is the greatest of Spanish philosophers; in fact, of all those writers in Spain who have written about philosophy, from Seneca to Unamuno and Ortega y Gasset, the only constructive thinker to produce a complete system is Maimonides.

In some ways he agreed with Averroës—indeed Moslems thought Averroës a great deal too Jewish: he had gone over to the Jews, they said. Like Averroës, Maimonides held that there could be no real quarrel between religion and science; there could be no conflict between truths which are discerned by reason and those inculcated by revealed religion. The apparent conflict was due to misrepresentation. Maimonides, like any modern thinker, had also to face the problem of the nature of the universe. The solution he adopted was more or less the spherical universe of Aristotle, with the earth fixed in the centre and the heavens revolving round it, the heavenly bodies being set in concentric transparent spheres ('the nine enfolded spheres', Milton called them), which revolved carrying the heavenly bodies with them. The outermost sphere had been set in motion by God, while the others were kept turning by Angels, whom Aristotle had termed Intelligences. There are medieval miniatures showing the theory of Maimonides literally interpreted, with angels to 'turn the adamantine spindle round'; and the system has been familiar to European poets since the time of Dante.

As the Moslem power in Spain receded, the Jews came under the less tolerant rule of Christians, while the retreat of Islam meant that the language of learning ceased to be Arabic. But the philosophic thought of Moslems and Jews in Spain had one tremendous consequence in the Angelic Doctor, St. Thomas Aquinas; his treatise *Summa contra gentiles* was, in fact, intended to be the refutation of the Spanish thinkers. To Maimonides St. Thomas owed more, perhaps, than his admirers are ready to admit: the relation of reason to revelation, Divine attributes, God's knowledge, Providence, Creation, and the structure of the universe. And Thomas Aquinas took from Maimonides one idea in particular which appears again later in Spanish and Renascence thought: the idea of God as the Supreme Artist.

After the middle of the thirteenth century—after the final capture of Córdoba in 1236 and of Seville in 1248—there was nothing left to the Spanish Moslems except the kingdom of Granada and the adjacent coast.[1] The dynasty was Arab: Nasrite; the founder was Ibn Ahmar, and the Red King, Al-Ahmar,

---

[1] It included Gibraltar, which, though captured by Castile in 1309, was lost again to Granada after twenty-five years and occupied definitely by Spaniards only from 1462 to 1704.

lived in the Red Palace, the famous *al-hamrā'*, Alhambra, of Granada.

The Nasrite dynasty of Granada kept the throne for 250 years by astute diplomacy, playing off one Christian kingdom against another: Castile against Aragon. The motto of the dynasty, 'And no conqueror but God', may be seen inscribed again and again on the walls of the Alhambra; it was what the founder was said to have remarked one day on returning from helping a king of Castile to defeat a Moslem Spanish state. Finally, internal dissension and the quarrels of two royal ladies—'Aïsha, supported by the Abencerrages, and Zoraya by the Zegríes—combined with the union of Castile and Aragon (1474), made an independent Granada impossible, and it surrendered to Ferdinand and Isabel on 2 January 1492. It capitulated on terms; it did not surrender unconditionally. Ferdinand and Isabel guaranteed religious freedom to the Moslem inhabitants; but the ecclesiastical authorities soon began to have their way, and in 1499 Cardinal Ximénez forced the inhabitants to burn all their Arabic books. 'He wished,' Professor Nicholson says, 'to annihilate the record of seven centuries of Muhammadan culture in a single day'; or, as Richard Ford put it, 'he preferred to purify by fire rather than by water'.

This bonfire of books and subsequent forcible conversion of the Moriscos (as the converted Moslems were called) was against the terms of the treaty. It led to a series of revolts followed by further acts of repression. The Moriscos were forbidden to wear their proper clothes, or perform any of their traditional ceremonies. They were even expressly forbidden to

take baths; washing was a practice which the Holy
Office considered to be proof of heresy. 'The accused
was known to take *baths*, even in December. . . .'
Such evidence, alone, was almost enough to secure a
conviction. Expulsion, often proposed and as often
postponed—Philip II knew the value of putting things
off till to-morrow—was finally decreed under Philip III;
and between 1609 and 1611 the Moriscos of Valencia,
Castile, Andalusia, Aragon, and Catalonia were shipped
across to North Africa. They might only take with
them such property as they could carry, and even that
was sometimes confiscated before they embarked.
Some managed to come back in disguise. We remember Sancho Panza's friend, Ricote, the Morisco
shopkeeper in his village, who had hidden his money
and hoped eventually to be able to convey his wife and
daughter from Morocco (where they were living in
great poverty, for Morocco did not want the Spanish
refugees). It is curious to notice that he wished to
emigrate to Germany, 'for,' as Cervantes says, 'in
the greater part of that country there is liberty of
conscience'

It must be repeated that a considerable part of the
Moslem inhabitants of Granada were of purely Spanish
European descent; and this notwithstanding the fact
that they were not Christians but Moslems. That
fact—that they were in no sense Africans or 'Moors'
but heretical Europeans—accounts largely for the
bitterness of the Christian persecution. In Aragon,
however, and in some other parts, the Moslem population was more Oriental, more African by descent; they
consisted mainly of agricultural labourers, and the great
landlords, realizing what would happen if several

hundred thousand agricultural labourers were taken away, did all they could to prevent the expulsion. It was no use; much land slipped out of cultivation, and from that moment (some authorities say) the decline of Spain began.

The Moriscos were not driven out finally until 1614; and, in spite of prohibitive orders to the contrary, Arabic of a sort was still spoken in the Peninsula until then; that is, during the lifetime of Cervantes. So it could not have struck his contemporaries as fantastic or impossible when he declared that the original of *Don Quixote* was the work of a Moor, called (by some joke that has been forgotten) Sidi Hamet ben Engeli; and that it, too, had originally been written in Arabic.

CHAPTER III

THE CHRISTIAN KINGDOMS

NORTH of the Pyrenees, in the early Middle Ages, civilization was being built up again by three great constructive forces: the Church, the Frankish kingdom, and the Feudal System. In Christian Spain, the Church was the only stable and far-reaching force capable of holding the quarrelsome Christians together, in the early years of the Reconquest, and welding the country into some kind of unity and cohesion. During eight centuries, while the Moslems were driven back, 'unoccupied Spain' spread gradually from the frontiers of Asturias over the centre, east, and west of the Peninsula; but it was not a single political organism. Even in the thirteenth century, when it coagulated into the three main blocks of Aragon-Catalonia, León-Castile, and Portugal, these three kingdoms still contained great diversities of custom, economy, and law.

After the Moslem conquest, Christian Spain had been confined to the wild mountainous country of the north and west, for the most part in districts where the town life of the Roman Empire had hardly developed at all. Then, as now, the inhabitants of Asturias and Galicia were scattered in small groups rather than collected into cities; and 'unoccupied Spain' at first consisted of empty wastes with small oases where crops were grown by serfs. The Reconquest of Spain from the Moslems is dated from the exploits of the Christian King Pelayo (died 737) in the Cave of Covadonga, in Asturias. These exploits have led to many lyrical and patriotic effusions; but it is difficult, at this distance of time, to see what the importance of this first encounter with the Moslems really was. Transfigured by the panegyrics of the chroniclers, it has become a national Spanish legend, a sonorous sacred name; and as such it can be accepted. But in the days of Covadonga the engagement may have been nothing but a successful counter-attack on a small raiding party. That, as any soldier will admit, is a respectable ancestry for a great nation; but it is a mistake to think that it was accompanied, at the time, by any national consciousness. The men of Covadonga were not aware of Spain as something lost or regained; all they knew was the personal ascendancy of their leader, the pride of their Visigothic ancestry, and the security of their Christian faith.

For the Church there was only one possible and permissible view of the Moslems. It was a doctrinal question. The Moslems were infidels; and though Christians might trade with them or even learn from them (the fact that a man had studied with the Moslems at Córdoba was no bar to his election as Pope) the first duty of the Church and its followers was either to convert them or, if not, to destroy them. In theory, there could be no compromise. Later on, when the Moslem Spaniards had submitted, the Christian Spaniards would refer to them as 'people who are not of our law'. By this they meant not the law of the law-books: not the Visigothic *Fuero Juzgo* (Forum Judicum or Court of Judges), nor the *Siete Partidas* (Seven Divisions), the legal code of Alfonso the Sage; nor yet the *fueros* (chartered rights) of the towns, nor the ecclesiastical canon law of the Church. By 'our law' they meant the moral law: our way of

thinking. From the days of the Reconquest down to
recent times, people of Spanish origin have always
regarded their politics as a moral question, and one on
which there is no possibility of concession. The
Spanish language still has no word for compromise, as
John Morley understood it.

That was the doctrine of the matter, and doctrine is
never without effects on living and action. But the
medieval gulf between theory and practice—the gulf
between the 'City of God' and the warring schisms of
the Church on earth, between the name of the Holy
Roman Empire and its real nature—was apparent in
Spain as elsewhere. There was no insincerity, no
mere 'convenance avec le ciel': only the results of an
attempt to believe in absolute standards while living
in a busy, humorous, and not intolerant world which
enjoyed a great measure of intellectual security. This
was a world in which the Spanish poet Berceo—a
contemporary of St. Francis of Assisi—could tell the
following story in praise of the Virgin Mary. In a
certain convent there was a Mother Abbess, who was
good and kind and charming; but she made one slip,
and found herself pregnant. When her condition
became obvious, her cattish nuns informed the Bishop,
who came to the convent to investigate. But on
the eve of his visit the Virgin arrived, delivered the
Abbess, and took the baby to a hermit near by; while
the Abbess, to the confusion of the nuns, appeared
before the Bishop 'as slender as a plank'. To a stiffer,
less human religion, such a story would have seemed
shocking or even blasphemous.

Berceo lived in the broad, kindly daylight of the
Spanish Church, far removed from that murky atmo-

sphere in which some of the Renascence mystics devised cruelties for themselves and their fellows. So, before religion was turned into a red-hot political weapon of Renascence kings or queens, Spanish Christians found ways of living side by side with their Moslem or Jewish neighbours. Spain, in Roman times, had seen a slow fitting together of many different races, a fusion of blood and spirit. Then, during seven centuries while Moslems lived in the country, there were times of friction and unrest, but there were also times of co-operation and understanding. In 'occupied Spain', Christians, Jews, and Moslems frequently intermarried. In Toledo, in the thirteenth century, the church of Santa María la Blanca was used for worship by all three religions: Christians on Sunday, Jews on Saturday, Moslems on Friday. Whatever their creed, all these people were becoming Spanish. The idea that a Spaniard must be, and could only be, a Christian was a later and less tolerant notion, a piece of special pleading which has distorted the facts to fit a political theory. There were medieval Christian thinkers (as Asín Palacios has shown) who even went so far as to regard Islam as a new and heretical form of Christianity, not a pagan creed. This may not have been common, but it shows that Spanish medieval history cannot be understood in the crude terms of the *Reconquista*. Such a view was based on a false racial unity and a slippery religious conformity, of which the ultimate consequences were to be the expulsion of Jews and Moslems, the annihilation of religious reformers, and the repression of Basques and Catalans —the domination, in fact, of the people of the plateau over the peoples of the coasts.

As time went by the Mozárabes—the Christians living in those parts of Spain which were ruled by Moslems—came to differ considerably from the independent northern Christians in religion, language, architecture, and music. A curious example may be found in the history of the music of the Liturgy, or form of church service. The Mozarabic rite is of considerable interest to scholars, by reason of its strange formulae and passionate mariolatry; but it seemed very near heresy to the more orthodox Christians from unoccupied Spain or from France. Queen Constance, first wife of Alfonso VI, was a Frenchwoman, and naturally wished to hear in church the music of her own country; for French music at the end of the eleventh century and the beginning of the twelfth had reached, in the school of Notre-Dame of Paris, one of the great periods of its history. But the Queen had forgotten to reckon with the Spanish character. A Castilian knight, Juan Ruiz de Matanzas, disapproved of the new customs; he offered to defend the old order and the old music against all comers, and in single combat he overthrew a French knight who had taken up the challenge to modern French music. It was then decided that the choice between the two liturgies, Mozarabic and Gallican, should be submitted to the Ordeal by Fire, and copies of the two prayer-books were duly committed to the flames. The Mozarabic service-book miraculously leapt from the fire; but the King kicked it back again with the remark: '*Allí van leyes do quieren reyes*' (laws go as kings will), and the Gallican rite was adopted in Spain.

What is remarkable in this story is not the tough behaviour of Alfonso VI, which has its parallel in every

age, but the action of the Castilian knight in risking
his life for a form of church music. That was something new in Europe, a contribution which we should
now call distinctively Spanish. It recalls the tale of
Suero de Quiñones, hero of the exploit known as the
paso honroso, who with a few chosen companions (but
with no apparent reason) held a bridge on the Pilgrims'
Way against all comers for thirty days in the summer
of 1434. Again, it reminds one of the seventeenth-
century gentleman from Seville, who challenged to
single combat any who should doubt the Immaculate
Conception. Such behaviour, for which courage and
devotion are altogether inadequate descriptions, is
known from its greatest and most famous exponent
as 'quixotic'. Mozarabic music (so far as it can be
read now) seems less melodious than Gregorian and
far less exciting than the school of Notre-Dame; the
paso honroso took place in time of peace; and the
Immaculate Conception was not proclaimed a dogma
until the time of the picturesque nineteenth-century
Pope, Pius IX, when its quixotic defender had been
dead for two hundred years. Yet practical uselessness
or apparent failure are among the noblest qualities of
Spanish quixotism. It is one of the rare attributes
of the race which arose in Spain in isolation from the
rest of Europe and seven hundred years' division against
itself—a division which was barely ended in one
direction when it began again in another, and has
continued to this day.

For the Christian Spaniards in general however
the medieval period was an age of epic rather than
of chivalry. The chivalrous ideal, mirrored in King
Arthur and the Knights of the Round Table, arrived

in Spain late, and arrived from Portugal and France. But the story of Roderick the Goth, who lost Spain to the Moslems, has many epic qualities and was the subject of lost heroic poems. So too was the tale of the Seven Infantes (Princes) of Lara, led into an ambush by the jealousy of an aunt and the machinations of a wicked uncle. The Moslems appear in the part of civilized though helpless onlookers at the spectacle of Christian barbarity. They were then the dominant power in the Peninsula, and the one which quarrelsome 'Balkanized' states tried to involve in every family vendetta.

By the tenth century, and still more in the eleventh, the historical conditions had begun to change. From the warring, Christian states of northern Spain had emerged, beside the more conservative and traditionalist León, the vigorous, innovating 'county' (*condado*) of Castile, which produced a great if legendary hero in Fernán González (*fl.* 950). This territory was a border region, always open to attack from Moslems coming up from the South; and the astute count profited by the anarchy of León and his own successes against the Moslems to make himself independent. Legends, ballads, and a later monkish poem, all give him an exciting career: how a princess got him out of prison on condition that he would marry her; how his own subjects, unable to agree in his absence, caused a statue of him to be carved and carried with them to remind them of his rule. But the most characteristic legend is one describing how he gained independence from the kingdom of León. Summoned to a meeting of the Cortes, he rode thither on so fine a horse and with so beautiful a hawk on his wrist that the king insisted on buying them; and though offered them as a gift, declared that he would pay the full price, which, he said, should be doubled for every day that passed after the money was due. Years went by and the money was not paid, until at last the sum had reached a figure so far beyond a medieval mind to compute, or a medieval king to pay, that the count could only be rewarded with the independence of his county of Castile. To a modern mind this story, which suggests that the leading state of Spain was born of a piece of Spanish unpunctuality, is typical rather than true.

The sons of Fernán González met with serious reverses from the Moslems, and his grandson was murdered on his wedding journey to León by the family of a certain Count Vela of Navarre. Thereupon León made war upon Navarre, taking care that the fighting should happen mainly in Castile; and at length the first king of Castile as an independent state was Ferdinand I, the son of a king of Navarre and an infanta of León. Yet the stubborn tradition of Castile, and the tough persistence of the Castilian people, prevailed in the end, along with the vigorous and emphatic Castilian dialect. Vigour and emphasis became characteristic features of the Castilian people. The emphatic quality of their speech has been pointed out by Spanish writers, from Seneca to Unamuno. Where Latin says *fŏrum*, Spanish says *fuero*; and the men who by shouting and over-emphasis could convert Latin short vowels into Castilian diphthongs were not likely to accept dictation from the less clear-spoken inhabitants of other districts. The Castilians developed a sense of leadership. Ferdinand became king of León as well as of Castile, and occupied the kingdom of

Navarre as far as the Ebro; but he left behind him the memory of a ruler who was also a lawgiver (*el de los buenos fueros*). At the Council of Coyanza (1050) he reintroduced Visigothic laws which had fallen into abeyance, tightened up ecclesiastical discipline, and confirmed the *fueros*—the chartered rights granted to subjects—already bestowed by his predecessor, Alfonso V of León. Yet even Ferdinand I made the fatal mistake of treating his kingdoms as personal property and dividing them among his children. The result was that the eldest son, Sancho, set about regaining his father's possessions by force, while the younger sons, Alfonso and García, fled to Moslem courts to plot their brother's downfall. One sister, Doña Elvira, submitted; and the only member of the family to resist was the stout-hearted Doña Urraca (Lady Magpie), to whom, as an afterthought, her father had bequeathed the lordship of Zamora.

At this point we make the acquaintance of Ruy Díaz de Bivar, the *Cid*: the great champion of Christian Castile who is known nevertheless by a title which is Arabic (*sīdī*, my Lord). His earliest adventures are the subject of innumerable ballads, and the modern investigation of his career involves folk-lore, comparative religion, and primitive superstition, as well as the more normal channels of historical and literary research. It is related that young Ruy Díaz killed a neighbouring landowner who had slighted his father, and that the enraged daughter then insisted on marrying her father's murderer—an episode only explicable from certain sections of *The Golden Bough*. On a subsequent occasion, a visit to the Pope of Rome, the Cid destroyed a precious ivory chair, either through clumsiness or to show that a Castilian was the equal of the greatest man in Christendom.

This however is mere legend. The historical Cid first appears at the siege of Zamora, in a subordinate position it is true, but more alert than his fellows, recognizing and trying to stop an assassin who had slipped into the camp and murdered the king. He only failed because his horse was not saddled and he had to ride after the man bareback. Suspicion for the crime fell not so much on Doña Urraca as on her brother, who now became king of Castile, León, and Galicia, as Alfonso VI; and the Castilians, following the customary procedure in such cases, made the new king swear, before twelve good men and true, that he had had no concern in his brother's death. The oath (which counts as one of the great constitutional documents of medieval Spain) was administered in the church of Santa Gadea (St. Agatha) at Burgos. The Cid was present, and subsequent history shows that that was one of the things for which Alfonso VI never forgave him.

While nothing is more characteristic of medieval Castile than that an important constitutional document should have become the subject of a popular ballad, the ballads on the siege of Zamora show the stages through which the story passed before it became firmly rooted in the public mind. The epic manner in which the event is related in the chronicles of the thirteenth and fourteenth centuries leaves no doubt that the chroniclers had in their thoughts—or even before their eyes—a lost epic poem, comparable in length and interest with the epic which we still have, the *Poema de mio Cid*. Further, it is possible to see how, in process of conversion from the epic (as reflected in the prose chronicle) to the ballad (which many Spanish people still know by heart), the merely narrative passages have dropped out, leaving only the two main actors clearly before our eyes. To the makers and singers of the old Spanish ballads, the Cid and Doña Urraca had known each other as children, and she had at one time wanted to marry him. So when, before the siege began, King Sancho sends the Cid to negotiate the surrender of the town, the ballad leaves the military details for the personal relationship between the Cid and Doña Urraca; the view has become, as it were, a 'close-up'. The Spanish ballad-makers never sentimentalized their subjects, but they often concentrated a moment of vision on the private feelings of the persons most intimately involved, in a manner not surpassed by the Border ballads of Britain.

In most of the new Christian states the first kings were elected, though the succession always tended to become hereditary. In the Moslem states, on the contrary, the rulers were despots. The Moslems started from the theory that equality was conferred on all men by Allah, as a birthright; but in politics the equality remained theoretical. The Christians, starting from the obviously unequal grades of a more or less feudal society, evolved the conception of an equality conferred by law, in the person of the king granting *fueros* to his subjects. The Spanish peoples struggled for many centuries towards an ideal expressed in the well-known Spanish saying: *Del rey abajo ninguno* (or, King and Commons with no Lords between). Unfortunately absolute monarchy, when it came, in the sixteenth century, did not take quite the form that they intended.

The medieval king was not absolute. True, the faculty of legislation belonged to the Crown: *quod principi placuit vim legis habet* (the king's pleasure has the force of law). But already in the Visigothic period the famous legal code, the *Fuero Juzgo*, had laid it down that the king was king only if he did right (*Rex eris si recte facias: si non facias, non eris*). In Spain as elsewhere in Europe the first and most fundamental principle of medieval political thought was that all political authority was the expression of justice. The second great principle was that there could be only one source of political authority: the community or the people itself. The King of Castile or Aragon had two superiors, God and the Law—law not made by the prince or legislator, but expressing the habit and custom of the community's life. It followed that the King could not take action against the property or person of any of his subjects except by a process of law. This principle had been stated in Spain before it was incorporated in our *Magna Carta*. Alfonso IX swore to observe it in 1188, before the Cortes of León, and it was announced at the Cortes of Valladolid in 1299. By that time there would have been strong protests against any such act as we hear of in the earlier *Poema de mio Cid*, when Alfonso VI sends a message to the inhabitants of Burgos forbidding any citizen to harbour the Cid, who had been banished by him. The townsmen, and women too—*burgeses e burgesas*, as the poem says—had all appeared at the windows (slits with no glass in them) to see the Cid ride through the town to exile, accompanied by sixty mounted men with pennons fluttering from their lances. But they were so afraid of being seen speaking to him that they sent out a little girl, nine years old, to tell him what the King's commands were. She told him of a royal letter delivered the night before, 'with much secrecy, and sealed with a great seal'—*con grand recabdo e fuertemientre seellada*. None should receive the Cid into their houses: if they did so they would lose their homes and their possessions, and the eyes in their heads as well.

But if this royal behaviour was typical of the eleventh century, it was out of date a hundred years later. It is seldom remembered that representative government began not in England but in Spain. Alfonso the Chaste (791–842) already ruled with a council of magnates and prelates; and, later, these councils developed into *Cortes* (parliaments) with representatives of the three estates: lords spiritual and temporal, and burgesses—bishops, nobles, and townsmen. The Cortes of León dates from 1188, while the Cortes in Aragon (with four estates instead of three) met even earlier. We are told that Doña Petronila, the heiress of Aragon and wife of the Count of Barcelona, summoned to Cortes in the city of Huesca 'the prelates, nobles, gentlemen, and the representatives from the towns' in the year 1162. Whether they came to Huesca or not, it is certain that they were present at the Cortes of Saragossa in the following year—132 years before the first English parliament of 1295.

Spanish municipalities were of mixed origins. Most of them had been there since Roman times or before; but some were Visigothic foundations, or had sprung up suddenly wherever there was a good chance of buying or selling, or a strategic position for defending territory gained from the Moslems. The early

independent Christians of the state of Asturias were
increased in course of time, not only by reconquest
and by Mozarabic immigrants, but also by wholesale
deportation of the inhabitants (Christian and Moslem)
from the towns and fortresses captured by the Asturian
kings but afterwards evacuated. The new arrivals
were men of many different types and social conditions.
There were free men who went to live in towns because
life there was less precarious, less monotonous, and
more independent than it was out in the country.
There were freed slaves who had somehow acquired
full personal liberty, with disposal of their own possessions and the right to live where they chose. There
were pedlars settling down as small traders. All
these came to the towns for greater safety and the help
of their neighbours against oppression; and there was
also the attraction of a share in civil and political rights
and the chance of making a better living.

When ground was conquered from the Moslems,
and the original inhabitants had been killed or enslaved,
these towns urgently needed repopulating. Life in
such places was still dangerous, and the kings granted
fueros to any colonists who had the courage to go and
live in them. Runaway slaves could take refuge from
pursuit in these districts, and were recognized as
citizens. A *fuero* of 1073 assures 'any who had
suffered ill-treatment under a bad master' that they
might come if they wished to Burgos or to certain
villages in the neighbourhood, and settle there with
all their goods and chattels (*cum omni reptile et mobile
suo*) under the same *fuero* as anybody else. Some of
the oldest and most liberal *fueros* included Jews and
Moslems as well as Christians: the *fuero* of Miranda

(1099) expressly states that it applies to all the inhabitants, Moslems or Jews. Berceo, in his Song of the Jews watching the body of Christ lest it should be stolen, uses the refrain *Eya velar!* (Hiya! Look out!) This is the Spanish for *Eia vigila!*—the watchmen's cry on the walls of Modena in an early medieval Latin poem. It must often have been cried by the Jews who went, with slaves and all kinds of vagabonds, to settle and guard the dangerous frontier towns of Christian Spain.

One of the privileges granted to certain communities in those unsettled regions was curious, and peculiar to Spain. The places called *behetrías* (*benefactorias*) were allowed to choose their own lord, and to change him for another if they were no longer content with him. Sometimes the choice was limited to a single noble family or to a particular district; other places could take a lord from anywhere in Spain (*behetrías de mar en mar*: from one sea to the other). This privilege, originally bestowed because of the urgent need of inducing men to people the newly annexed territories, was too sharply incompatible with feudal ideas to appeal either to the king or to the nobility in safer times; and it eventually fell into disuse through royal ordinances forbidding any noble to reside in a *beheiria*.

Some of the Spanish towns had a trained militia, a Home Guard, of their own. Most of them were getting rich on industry and commerce. As they grew large and strong they began to demand more than the limited powers of local administration which were possible under the lordship of a noble or a monastery: control of food and marketing, the right to use roads and bridges and the duty to pay for their upkeep.

Gradually the town council acquired powers of acting by itself, especially in the administration of justice; and through these the *fueros*, the rights and liberties of the towns, developed and were defined by charter.

Much the same thing happened in other medieval towns of Europe, but in Spain it had special features. Where did the Spanish town council come from? Some historians have thought that it came down from Roman times; for the Roman *municipium*, or chartered town, also had a council, and the two chief magistrates (*duoviri*) of Roman towns have been compared with the Spanish *alcaldes*, or mayors, who are sometimes found in couples. But there is a break in continuity: the *duoviri* no longer exist in Visigothic times, nor are they found among the Mozárabes. However, there is no need to look for origins in the Roman Empire; the Iberian municipal council is much older. Something like the primitive gathering of townsmen has even survived in modern times: it was to be heard of in out-of-the-way villages in this century, and often took place during the civil war of 1936–39. The Spanish scholar Hinojosa believed that this native gathering turned into the Visigothic judicial council, and then into the medieval council of the independent municipality. The authority of the noble landowner was probably replaced inside the town boundary by an elected judge; and the magistrates, instead of being appointed by the lord, were elected as mayors by a popular vote for the term of one year. These things are interesting because they show that the Spanish people, before absolute monarchy interfered with their liberties, were not by any means so lacking in political sense as they are sometimes supposed to be. On the contrary, they were perfectly capable of running their own affairs, and of creating progressive institutions for themselves.

In León and Castile the democratically elected town council, with its own juridical powers, came into existence about 1220. Its *fuero* established the equality before the law of all citizens within its boundaries. Henceforth it was a privileged and more or less autonomous body recognized by the King. But towns which were subject to an ecclesiastical lord—a church or a monastery—instead of a secular noble holding his authority from the Crown, had a longer and sharper struggle for their rights of independence. Santiago de Compostela, the place of pilgrimage from all Europe, led the way in the fight against ecclesiastical government. The Cathedral Chapter and the City Council often came to blows: some of the clergy took sides against the dictatorial Archbishop Gelmírez, who found a bonfire lighted on his staircase one day and barely escaped with his life. Princess Urraca, daughter of Alfonso VI of Castile and a niece of the Cid's Doña Urraca, spent most of her stormy life in Santiago, raging between her husband and her lovers or intriguing with the Archbishop. The citizens caught her and stripped her naked for flouting both their moral convictions and their political rights. In Sahagún the townsmen rose against the Benedictine Abbey, expelled the Abbot, and trampled on his vineyards and his vegetables.

It is easy to see why these struggles were especially bitter in towns under the lordship of the Church. The lay lords, as a rule, resided at court—wherever the wandering medieval court might happen to be; they followed their king on his military expeditions, or lived as robber-barons in their castles. At any rate, they were not often visible, and were not in constant and irritating contact with the inhabitants of the towns under their control. The ecclesiastical lords, on the contrary—the bishops and abbots—lived permanently in the towns subject to their jurisdiction; and when they defended their privileges against the unifying, levelling tendencies of the town councils there arose antagonism or civil strife of far greater violence than usually occurred in towns of which the lords were laymen.

It was difficult for the clergy to renounce the privileged position which they held in medieval Spanish society. They did not form part of the bourgeoisie; they existed alongside of it. Privileges of the *fuero* relieved them from a good many of the restrictions of civil legislation. A privilege granted to Toledo by Alfonso VII in 1136 forbade the law officers (who still kept the Castilianized Arabic name of *zalmedina*) to enter the houses of any of the clergy; and if any layman had a case against a cleric he had to go before a bishop's court and receive judgement according to ecclesiastical law. The *fuero* of Salamanca had a provision in the same sense. The clergy were thus exempt from municipal law-courts, while their royal immunity relieved them from most of the charges which weighed upon other citizens. The *Fuero de los Mozárabes, Castellanos y Francos de Toledo* declared that all clergy who took duty by night as well as by day should hold their lands free of taxation. Not only those goods which were the property of the Church were free from municipal contributions, but also the private possessions of those in holy orders. Domestic and rural dependants of ecclesiastics often enjoyed the same personal exemptions as their masters. By the vexatious right of *mañería*, the lord inherited the property of a man dying without issue. A monopoly of the sale of wine also belonged to the lord. What probably annoyed the townsfolk most of all was the right of precedence in marketing: they were kept waiting in queues until the monks had done their own shopping. Against all these privileges the municipalities strove—with gradual or partial success—to establish one *fuero* for all and to gain equal economic opportunity.

The *fueros* arose out of the actual needs of men and women in the Middle Ages. They were not the arbitrary creation of lawyers, or derived from existing codes and systems. They reflect the life and ideas of the times as the various questions came up for discussion in popular assemblies or municipal tribunals. They reflect also the practical autonomy which the common townsfolk of Christian Spain had to win for themselves—whereas in Moslem Spain, for all its doctrines of equality, municipal officers, police, and Clerks of the Market were appointed from above, and not elected by the town itself. The *fueros* are a crystallized deposit of the thoughts and feelings, the private lives and public institutions, the agriculture, industry, and commerce, and indeed the whole social, political, and economic life of Spain in the early Middle Ages. They show those early generations, to whom Spain owed such great political and administrative progress, struggling to defend their independence, first against the Moslem invaders and then against the haughty

Castilian magnates; running up their fortifications and enrolling their home guard to resist aggression from any power that threatened their way of life.

In the *fueros* we can see the townsfolk going to market, buying and selling, quarrelling over weights and measures, protesting if an importunate friar tried to be served first; it should be the same for all, they declare, friar or layman, or the turbaned stranger 'not of our law', who had just come in from one of the outlying villages. They pushed and sweated, pointed and shouted; and along with their municipal institutions they developed their language and their literature. What does that early literature give us? A set of scenes, clear and unforgettable as the panels of a primitive painting. In the din and clatter of a crowded market-place a minstrel plucks a stringed instrument and bawls an endless story of the Cid, the Seven Princes of Lara, or the Magpie Lady of Zamora. A mysterious cleric, who says that he is a minstrel of the lord, tells rhymed stories of local saints and mundane miracles, adding that he thinks them well worth a glass of good wine. Under the wooden portico of a municipal building an Archpriest chats quietly with a malicious old woman and watches a pretty young widow tripping across the square:

> *Ay Dios, e quan fermosa viene*
> *doña Endrina por la plaza!*

The Archpriest of Hita has been called the Chaucer of Spain. He is comparable to Chaucer, both in humour and in poetic genius. His *Libro de buen amor* (Book of the Love of God) is actually a book of the love of women, though the Archpriest carefully explains that he recounts the incidents as an example

to be avoided. He recounts them, however, with
great gusto and with a wealth of practical advice. After
a discourse on the arms with which a true Christian
should resist the world, the flesh, and the devil, he
proceeds straight to a passage of elaborate arguments
contending that small women are the best. Yet he
has too much human interest to become pornographic,
and too much wit to be gross. Whether his book is
autobiographical or not, he wrote about people—the
Spanish people of his time. Not only the canons of
Talavera and the lecherous milkmaids of Segovia, but
also the animals of medieval fable, or Don Amor and
Doña Venus, and Lord Carnival and Lady Lent, are
all characters of flesh and blood who talk, argue, and
answer each other back. The Archpriest lived half
a century earlier than Chaucer, but the difference
between them is not so much a difference of time as
of social background. Chaucer was a man of the
metropolis, and a good European; the Archpriest
belonged to a Spanish country town, and his people
are of the market-place, the fields, and the sierras.
They were the busy people described earlier in the
poem of the Cid:

> Now the dawn is cracking,
>   and soon it is the morning.
> Up came the sun,
>   Lord! How lovely in his rising!
> In Castejón town
>   they leave their beds behind them,
> Open the house doors,
>   and leap across the doorstep;
> Off to see their ploughed fields,
>   and all their possessions.

Beyond the town walls were the vast empty spaces of

plain and mountain: the communal agriculture which the *fueros* encouraged, the communal woodlands which were only cut down later when they became private property, the fruit which could be grown whenever the community brought the water and the Moslems showed them how to manage it. The men who knew how to grow wheat on the plains of Castile, apricots in the *cigarrales* of Toledo, oranges in the *huertas* of Valencia, did as much for the welfare of Spain as all the grand captains whose ideas began and ended with conquest. But even the grand captains came from country towns; and the Cid, a citizen who knew the law and was the owner of a water-mill, was for those very reasons a typical Castilian of his time. The medieval Castilian town was a country town, depending on agriculture and the law, farming and the *fuero*.

Before the emergence of an independent Castile, Spain was divided not only between Christians and Moslems but also between Cantabrian peoples and Pyrenean peoples. The *Reconquista* did not begin only with Pelayo in the Cave of Covadonga. Attempts were made in isolated parts of the Pyrenees, and these Pyrenean points of resistance gradually evolved into the kingdom of Aragon and the county of Barcelona The mountain chieftains in the Pyrenees saw the necessity for joining forces under a single leader, and chose a king, imposing on him definite conditions for holding that office. There was therefore a fundamental difference between the early Spanish monarchies in the Asturias and those in the Pyrenees: in the one, the king had been raised above all the other chiefs; in the other, the chiefs considered themselves every whit as good as the monarch, though by common consent he had been placed in command. The Catalan-Aragonese monarchy was always assumed to be based upon a pact or contract between King and People.

The title of King of *Aragon* survived as an official description of the states over which his sovereignty extended, while *Catalan* was used to designate the greater part of his subjects. Thus, though their flag became known as 'the bars of Aragon', the men who carried it from one end of the Mediterranean to the other were Catalans; and it was remarked by a medieval chronicler, and repeated by a nineteenth-century poet, that not a fish dared show itself in the Mediterranean without having the bars of Aragon on its tail. The Catalans drew up a special code of maritime law (*Consolat de mar*), in advance of any existing at the time, and made their influence felt far from the coast of Spain: Mallorca (1229), Menorca, Ibiza, Valencia, Sicily (1282), and also (though the conquest was never completed) Sardinia and Tunis. The Catalan language —and also, it is said, Catalan songs—are still to be heard at Alghero on the west coast of Sardinia, and a variety of Catalan is spoken at Valencia and in the Balearic Isles.

At the end of a later war in Sicily (1302) the king (who was brother to the King of Aragon) suggested to Roger de Flor, the commander of a Catalan expeditionary force, that he should take his troops to Constantinople to help the Byzantine Emperor against the Turks. Roger agreed; and in Sicilian ships they were conveyed to the Sea of Marmora. But after an initial success against the Turks they were treacherously attacked by some of the Byzantines who had engaged them, and Roger de Flor with many of his captains and light-armed *almogávares* were killed. Catalan vengeance became proverbial. After a few difficult and anxious weeks in the neighbourhood of Gallipoli they attacked the Byzantines, looting and burning wherever they went. Called in by the Duke of Athens, they were again treacherously attacked; and their chronicler, Ramón Muntaner, remarks that the word of a Turk, though pagan, was worth more than that of a Christian Greek. They set up a new Duke of Athens: a Catalan, son of the king of Sicily; and the consequence of the military achievements of the 'Catalan Company' in Greece was the establishment of a new medieval state, governed by Catalan rulers (of the Sicilian branch) until the line ended in 1377. The Catalans of Athens then decided to place themselves under the protection of Peter IV of Aragon. They sent to Spain a deputation including Joan Boyl, the Catalan bishop of Megara. Boyl was a remarkable character, a member of a noble family whose arms are to be found on some of the finest lustre pottery made by the Moslems in Christian Spain. He seems to have been one of the few men of western Europe in his time who had any idea of what Greek civilization had meant. Since 1374, when an Italian adventurer of the family of the Acciajuoli had become lord of Corinth and turned him out of his diocese, Bishop Boyl had lived on the Acropolis at Athens, and knew the Parthenon when a great deal more of it was to be seen than at present. Phidias' great statue of Athene had already disappeared; and the north pediment, representing the birth of the goddess, had been destroyed by Byzantine reconstruction. But many of the sculptures which are now in the British Museum were in their original places. The west pediment was intact, showing the victory of Athene over the sea-god Poseidon; and most of the metopes were still there, displaying before the eyes of the Catalan bishop and his sentries the combats of gods and giants, Centaurs and Lapiths, Athenians and Amazons, together with the frieze of the Panathenaic procession. Boyl asked King Peter for a guard of ten or a dozen men for so priceless a possession; and the king's instructions to the Treasurer are preserved in a document in the Archives of the Crown of Aragon at Barcelona. The guard seemed most necessary, he said, and should be sent without fail; for the said castle (the Acropolis) was 'the richest jewel there is in the world'. Other early travellers remarked that the 'Castle of Athens' was a good fortress; but it was a Catalan who first noticed that it was beautiful.

The line of Catalan and Aragonese kings ended with Martin I in 1410; his son had died before him. There were several claimants to the throne, and it was agreed by the separate Cortes of Aragon, Catalonia, and Valencia to hold a general meeting at Caspe, to decide on Martin's successor. The claimant most favoured in Barcelona was the Count of Urgell; but he was in too much of a hurry and spoilt his chances. One of the members of the meeting was the famous preacher, San Vicente Ferrer, and it was probably due to his influence (acting on behalf of the Avignon Pope, Benedict XIII) that the election fell to a Castilian: Ferdinand, a nephew of the last two kings of Aragon, known from a famous military exploit against the Moslems of Granada as 'the Man of Antequera'. At the time of the election of Caspe, Ferdinand was acting as regent for the boy-king of Castile, Juan II. He was a man of great personal integrity, and had been shocked and disillusioned, during the preparations for the attack on Antequera, by the behaviour of the Castilian nobles: they had drawn more pay than was due for the number of men under arms, and seemed to regard the *Reconquista* as a business proposition, using a crusade against the Moslems as a means of making money and cheating the Crown in every possible way.

By the election of Caspe Ferdinand of Antequera succeeded to the throne of Aragon. There was nothing against him, except that he was a Castilian. 'Ferdinand and his Castilians are not free, as we are', a Catalan historian remarked ten years afterwards; and there is no doubt that there were features in Ferdinand's political education which clashed with the ancient customs of Aragon and Catalonia. His first Cortes (1414) denied him supplies, complaining that he had introduced Castilians into the country as his agents. Ill and crestfallen, he returned to Barcelona, and found that, instead of receiving a subsidy, he was expected to pay the rates, like anyone else in the city. Ferdinand at first refused; whereupon Joan Fivaller, one of the five municipal councillors, waited on the king and informed him that the councillors were ready to lose their lives rather than break the municipal *fuero*. The rates were paid, but Ferdinand died on the road back to Castile.

The extinction of the Catalan dynasty on the throne of Aragon embittered certain outstanding disputes between the nobles and the king. These disputes came to a head half a century later in a destructive peasants' revolt, the revolt of the *Remenses*. The social

system of Catalonia seems to have shown a greater
sense of equality than there was in Castile, especially
in the towns, where municipal liberty, and a more
equal division of wealth than prevailed in other parts
of Spain, had caused society to develop more rapidly.
Political sense was native to most of the House of
Aragon: they had an acute perception of the realities
of a situation, a mixture of prudence and firmness,
which are two of the ingredients of a characteristic
Catalan quality, *seny*—a word expressing something
more restricted than 'sense', but more subtle than
'commonsense'.

The political sense of the towns, however, was by no
means shared by many of the country landlords, and
some of the Catalan agricultural labourers were worse
off than any in Castile, especially those known as
pagesos de remensa. The institution of *pagesia de
remensa* was a combination of the Roman agricultural
colonate, binding a man to the land he cultivated, and
the personal obligation introduced by the Visigoths
and Franks. Even the name *remensa* (Latin *redemptio*,
or *redimentia*) meant that it was legally impossible for
a man to leave the land on which he worked without
paying 'redemption', which was usually assessed at
one-third of all the movable property he possessed.
His only remedy was to escape and live ' for a year,
a month, and a day' in a privileged place, such as
Barcelona. If a *pagès* died leaving no male heir, his
family had to hand over to the landlord a portion
equivalent to what a son's portion would have been.
If his wife committed adultery, half her personal
belongings were forfeit. If a building caught fire, the
pagès had to compensate the landlord to the extent of

one-third of his goods. The lord also possessed vexatious rights of interference in the life of the *pagès*'s family: he could take his wife as a wet nurse and his daughters for domestic servants; when the *pagès* died he could remove the best blanket in the house, and he could claim (like the Count in *Figaro*) the feudal *droit de seigneur* over a bride on the night before her marriage.

In 1462 members of the Catalan Cortes and the City Council of Barcelona made serious proposals for a settlement. When these were rejected by the land-owners, the *pagesos* broke out in open insurrection, which flared up again with peculiar violence in 1475. It is here that we make the acquaintance of Ferdinand the Catholic, husband of Isabel of Castile. He makes his first appearance settling a labour dispute, and his settlement (1486) was described at the time as 'one of the things in which the Catholic king had most conspicuously shown his valour and prudence'. Acting as far as he could in the interests of the *pagesos*, he won for them almost complete emancipation, fixing a definite and relatively small quota so that nearly all could purchase their redemption. The award was not very different from that proposed in 1462; but by this time both nobles and *pagesos* had suffered irreparable loss, for the revolt of the *remenses* had ruined agriculture and was one of the main causes of the decline of Catalonia.

Other reasons brought forward to explain this decline take us into a psychological and temperamental controversy which can never be settled. Catalan writers, beginning as early as the fifteenth century and the election of Ferdinand of Antequera,

blame the coming of a Castilian to the throne of
Aragon. Their complaints are only intensified by the
marriage of Ferdinand of Aragon to Isabel of
Castile (1469) and Ferdinand's succession to the
crown of Aragon (1479). Ferdinand of Antequera
had been the son of a king of Castile and an *infanta*
of Aragon; Ferdinand the Catholic was the son of
the last king of Aragon and the daughter of an
almirante of Castile. There was not only a change
of dynasty; there was a change in the whole conception of monarchy. Ferdinand came nearer than
any other Spanish ruler to the ideal prince portrayed
by Machiavelli: the type of Renascence despot; and
that did not suit those peoples which had preserved
their medieval privileges and hoped still to enjoy
them in the new, unified, renascent state of Spain.

Catalonia and Aragon received another blow: the
fall of Constantinople to the Turks (1453). Catalan
sea-power came to an end. The Mediterranean
grew unsafe for Christian ships. Watch-towers had
to be built every twenty miles along the shore, and
shipping was obliged to hug the coast to avoid falling
into the hands of the Moslems who now had command
of the sea. Position after position fell: Otranto, Corfu,
Durazzo, Rhodes, Cyprus. Trade with the Levant
became impossible. Nor did the discovery of America
bring any advantage to Catalonia in this respect.
Barcelona was on the wrong side of Spain for trade
with the Indies, and the primacy among Spanish ports
passed to Seville.

CHAPTER IV
MONARCHY AND EMPIRE

THE states of medieval Spain existed as separate units because Spain was a land of great natural variety, falling into clearly defined regions divided by mountains. But by the end of the fifteenth century it was clear that Spain must choose between the examples of France and Italy: to be a great, independent, unified nation, or to be a mere geographical expression without political cohesion between its parts, constantly liable to civil wars and invasion from abroad. The schemes of the French kings were always a menace to their neighbours, as the Italian states found out when France invaded them in 1494. There was no hope of survival in Renascence times under the medieval system of separatism, especially for peoples bordering on France; and this danger was constantly present to the minds of King Ferdinand of Aragon and Queen Isabel of Castile, urging them to the conquest of the Moslem kingdom of Granada and the union of all the Peninsular states under their joint domination.

With the death of Henry IV of Castile in 1474 the Spanish Middle Ages ended. Isabel and the consort she had chosen for herself were proclaimed joint sovereigns; but the Queen could not succeed to the throne of Castile without first winning a war of succession. That, owing to intervention from Portugal, was not over until 1479, the year in which Ferdinand succeeded to the throne of Aragon. In that country, too, there had been a civil war, with intervention from France. The first thing brought to their distracted countries by 'the Catholic Sovereigns' (*los reyes católicos*, as Ferdinand and Isabel were called) was peace.

The end of these dynastic wars brought the peaceful opportunity of uniting Spain under the joint crown. It was also the occasion for the conquest of the last Moslem kingdom, Granada, which had been torn throughout the fifteenth century, no less than Castile and Aragon, by civil strife between pretenders to the Moslem throne. To the Catholic Sovereigns the question of Granada was not racial but religious. The reason for the conquest was that Spain, in proportion to its varieties and differences, needed a strong unifying force to weld it together; and that force came from religion. Many of the Moslems in Spain were of completely Spanish descent. Racial exclusiveness, in Spain and elsewhere, is derived from false history, false science, and false religion. Neither the Roman Empire nor Christianity had accepted the idea of innate inferiority or superiority in different peoples; and the Castilians, with their theory of purity of blood (*limpieza de sangre*) and the claim to be 'old Christians' (*cristianos viejos*), perverted both Christian tradition and Catholic doctrine. That was where the Tribunal of the Inquisition came in. It was set up at Seville, in its peculiarly ruthless and efficient Spanish form, in 1480, to examine the sincerity of Jewish converts. Its introduction must be laid at the door of Queen Isabel; but she received encouragement from the Pope (1483), and also no doubt from her consort, in whose Catalan and Aragonese dominions the Inquisition, in a less active form, had existed for many years. The new tribunal in Seville began practising those severities which have made its name, and that of the chief Inquisitor, Torquemada, a byword. It was concerned at first only with Jews and Moslems who had accepted Christian baptism; but the Holy Office, from being a weapon for use against heretics, soon became a sort of Gestapo for tracking down those persons who were politically indiscreet or inconvenient to the State.

In recent years, leniency towards the Inquisition has become fashionable among historians. It is urged that cruel things were done in other countries besides Spain, and that these events must be judged by the standards of the time. There is, of course, a measure of truth in this. What is false is the assumption that each age has only one set of standards: those of its government and of the thoughtless masses who accept current ideas without criticism. It is not true that the Inquisition was accepted or approved by the finest contemporary minds in Spain. Its persecution or suspicion fell upon many of those who are now regarded as the brightest lights of Christian thought, and upon many more whose faith was sincerely held. In the next chapter we shall speak of their attitude.

The Jews, with their international connexions and their wealth, were an easy prey. The persecution of a Jew will always achieve cheap popularity, and one of the least penalties imposed on Spanish Jews was the confiscation of property. The Moslems, on their side, professed a religion by which all men were equal in the sight of God and the Law, a dangerous heresy which no European ruler could tolerate. It has already been pointed out in an earlier chapter that Cardinal Ximénez, to whom Isabel entrusted the management of the Inquisition, broke the terms of the capitulation of

Granada by his repression of Moslems. The burning of Moslem books and the forced conversions, the persecutions and deportations, were morally a crime and economically the first of those ill-considered political actions which led to Spanish decadence. Juridically considered, they were no more defensible than the deportation of the Spanish Jews. They could only be justified as a political move; but their political value was assessed in terms of a religious gesture. Nothing is more absurd, or a greater falsification of history, than to describe these events as the culmination of a war of reconquest which had lasted ever since the defeat of Roderick the Goth in 711. It would be equally true to describe the British Parliament Act of 1911 and the abolition of the veto of the House of Lords as the last stage in a struggle against the hereditary privilege of intruding foreigners which began at the Norman Conquest in 1066. But Ferdinand and Isabel could not have done what they did, nor have made Spain an efficiently governed, modern, centralist state instead of an anarchic and anachronistic medieval one, without some strong ideological directing force; and the ideologies of the day were all of them religious. A nationalist, militant catholicism served as the intellectual and emotional cement of the new state. Judged by its material or strategic effects, the acquisition of Granada was no more important than the incorporation of Navarre into the new joint kingdom; but from the point of view of ideology, it was a symbol of Isabel's policy of a united Catholic Spain, ruthlessly carried out by Cardinal Ximénez de Cisneros.

When Ferdinand and Isabel had united most of the

Peninsula under their rule (their plans for Portugal came to nothing, and Navarre was only absorbed after Isabel's death) they had to deal energetically with disturbers of the peace. As in France and England, the power of the feudal lords had to be drastically curtailed. Realizing that force could only be eliminated if it were opposed by greater force, the Catholic Sovereigns turned to the Fraternities of Castile (*Hermandades de Castilla*) founded as a rural constabulary in 1466. From these they formed the police force called *Santa Hermandad* (the Holy Fraternity)— the very thought of which was enough to terrify Sancho Panza a hundred years later—and this became the mainstay of the power of the state, as Ferdinand and Isabel conceived it: an instrument for keeping order, not only among thieves and malefactors but also among the turbulent nobles who, for generations, had been accustomed to pursue their political aims with private armies. Ferdinand and Isabel adroitly converted them from territorial barons, living independently in their castles, to courtiers whose duty and distinction was to attend the king and queen.

This curtailment of the power of the great landlords earned the Catholic Sovereigns the sympathetic support of the townspeople; but in their administrative reforms they found it necessary to reduce municipal liberties as well. The Peninsular peoples had no sense of unity to give them a common interest in mutual defence; and Ferdinand and Isabel, living at the beginning of an age of sovereign, autocratic, national states, could not allow quaint and contradictory local privileges to endanger the order and security of the country as a whole. They were working for the survival of Spain as an independent nation, and wished to gather into the hands of the monarchy all the effective powers of the State. They set aside many municipal *fueros*, and appointed royal representatives (*corregidores*) to sit on town councils and royal auditors for the municipal accounts. The townspeople, however, remained firmly loyal; and from them the Catholic Sovereigns recruited their lawyers (*letrados*): men who had been educated in Roman law at the universities, and could be of service to Ferdinand and Isabel in their struggle with the nobility. Ferdinand meanwhile made drastic changes in the powerful municipality of Barcelona, in favour of the moneyed middle classes.

Parliaments were seldom summoned. During the period of greatest military and political activity in the joint reign, the Cortes of Castile never met once, and years went by without a meeting of the Cortes of Aragon, Catalonia, or Valencia. The chief function of the Cortes continued to be consultative and financial, rather than legislative: Ferdinand did not need Cortes, except for voting supplies; and the members, for their part, had far less need to protest than they were to have later on, under Charles V. Yet at each new accession, when a new monarch had to be proclaimed, the act of swearing to respect the *fueros* and liberties of the people still remained an important part of the ceremony; and the petitions presented by the *procuradores*, or municipal representatives, converted the Cortes into a means of direct communication between the people and the king. Cortes were also summoned when the king wished to invest a decision of his own with more importance, or present it as the

general agreed opinion of his subjects. In Castile and
Aragon, as in England, legislation belonged theoretic-
ally to the King in Parliament; but Spanish parliaments, perhaps because they always remained local
assemblies (or had the character of local assemblies),
never became a fundamental part of the body politic.
They were an appendix to the royal power, not an
essential part of it; and even those stout Castilian
parliamentarians who afterwards protested so vigorously
to Charles V seem to have had little idea that they
could ever come to control his policy. It was this,
rather than that they never had an idea of the meaning
of liberty (as the historian Buckle thought), which
deprived the Cortes of any initiative in legislation.
Yet there can be no doubt that the new Monarchy
was supported by the people. Confidence accorded to
the government by the governed made the Spain of
Ferdinand and Isabel a living thing and a great
beginning. Ferdinand and Isabel increased the self-
respect, self-reliance, and self-sacrifice of their people.
In subsequent reigns that trust turned to cynicism,
hopelessness, and despair.

Like Tudor England, the new absolutist Spain was
full of intellectual and geographical adventure; even
its intolerance was alive and excited, energetic and
expansive. Ferdinand and Isabel were Spaniards, and
still close to their own peoples. The art and literature
of the time reflect popular life rather than the Court.
To Castilians, Isabel seemed one of themselves. With
her open, honest face, and her greenish-blue eyes (*los
ojos entre verdes e azules, el mirar gracioso e honesto*), she
had almost the look of a villager, or the inhabitant of a
small country town—as indeed she was, whether she

was actually born at Madrid, or in the little walled town which claims her as its citizen, and bears the splendid name of Madrigal de las Altas Torres. She had a good heart, and she had a fund of practical common sense, mixed with credulity, reverence, and a horror of witchcraft. With a few simple political ideas and great determination, she dreamed of a far happier Spain than the Hapsburg kings who succeeded her were to make of it: a political and religious union of all the Peninsular kingdoms, with command of the coast of North Africa from Oran to Tripoli (Naples and Sicily were the concern of Ferdinand). Most characteristic of her is her blunt question to the scholar Nebrija, when presented with his Spanish Grammar, the first grammar of a modern language ever written: 'What is it for?' And her greenish-blue eyes would have opened very wide at the portentous answer: 'Language is the perfect instrument of empire.'

Ferdinand, on the contrary, had nothing of the villager about him. Charming, erratic, one of the best horsemen of his time; with straight, black hair and laughing eyes, he was astute enough almost to get the better of a Catalan peasant, and politician enough to earn the approval of Machiavelli. He had, in fact, all the qualities (except cruelty) which in those days made the perfect prince. Louis XII of France complained that on two occasions Ferdinand had deceived him. 'He lies,' Ferdinand answered; 'I have deceived him not twice but ten times.'

In the spring of 1493 a high official of the Catholic Sovereigns received a letter from a Genoese merchant with the soul of a poet and the ambition to be an admiral: Christopher Columbus. The letter was written on board a caravel lying off the Azores:

'Señor: I know that you will take pleasure in the great success which Our Lord has given me on my voyage. I write you this letter that you may see that in 33 days I passed from the Canary Isles to the Indies with the fleet which the Most Illustrious King and Queen our sovereigns had been pleased to give me. There I discovered many islands inhabited by people without number; and I took possession of them all for Their Highnesses, by proclamation and hoisting the Royal Standard; and there was no other claimant. The first island that I found [Watling Island, Bahamas], I called San Salvador, and thus to every one I gave a new name. When I reached Juana, I sailed westward along the coast, and found it so long that I thought it must be the mainland: the province of Cathay [in China]. And as I could not find any towns or villages on the seashore, except small settlements—with the inhabitants of which I could have no speech, for they ran away immediately—I went forward on the same course, thinking that I should not fail to find great cities or towns. . . .

'I understood well enough from other Indians, whom by this time I had captured, that this land was an island; and so I followed the coast in an easterly direction for 107 leagues [428 miles] to where it ended. From that cape I saw another island to the east, about 18 leagues distant, to which I at once gave the name of Española [Haiti]. . . . This island and all the others are most fertile, to an excessive degree; and on this one the fertility is extreme. It has many harbours on the coast, beyond compare with others that I know in the

whole of Christendom; and enough rivers, both wide
and deep, which are a marvel. Inland, it is high; and
there are many ranges of mountains. . . . All these hills
are most beautiful; of a thousand shapes, all accessible,
and full of thousands of trees, so tall that they seem to
touch the sky; and I have heard it said that they never
lose their leaves, so far as I understand it. For I saw
them just as green and beautiful as they are in May in
Spain; and some of them were in flower and some in
fruit, and some between the one and the other according
to their kind. And the nightingale was singing, and
other small birds in thousands of kinds, in the month
of November when I was there. There are palms, of
six or eight different kinds—it is a wonder to see them,
for their astonishing beauty and variety; but so it is
with all the other trees and fruits and plants. There
are pine-woods which are a marvel, and wide open
spaces; there is honey, and many kinds of birds, and
fruits of many different sorts. . . . Altogether, Española
is a miracle. . . .'

Columbus felt like a traveller in a fairyland. He was
excited by all he saw, and struggled to put it into
words as best he could; there can be no doubt of his
sincerity. Yet he speaks of nightingales, which he
cannot have heard, for there are no nightingales in the
western hemisphere. The fact is that he could only
describe his adventures in the language of poetry: the
poetry which so many men before him had written
about the fabulous gardens of the Earthly Paradise,
which was actually supposed to lie beyond the western
ocean. When he heard the song of a bird, it could
only be the bird which sang in every description of the
Earthly Paradise: the nightingale.

The conquests became more businesslike, and more military; but the conquistadores seldom lost their sense of wonder and admiration. *Gracias le sean dadas, Señor, que me permites contemplar algo nuevo*: Thanks to thee be given, Lord, who permittest me to behold something new! Those were the sentiments of Juan Ponce de León, the discoverer of Florida; and they are implicit in the account of Cortés' march to Mexico, given by Bernal Díaz del Castillo:

'We set out from Cholula in marching order, as our custom was, the mounted patrols examining the country ahead, and very active men accompanying them on foot, so that if there should be any bad ground or obstacle, they might assist one another. Then came our guns ready for action; the musketeers, the crossbowmen; and the horsemen three a-breast so that they could support one another, and then all the rest of the troops in order of march. I do not know why I remember all this so clearly; but in things to do with war, we feel obliged to mention them, so that it may be seen how we went along, with our chins always over our shoulders. . . . We slept at a place . . . where half the houses were in the water and the other half on dry land, . . . and there they gave us a good supper. . . . And as we were always accustomed to post sentries and scouts, one of the scouts came in to tell us that a large crowd of friendly Mexicans was coming along the road, and that it seemed they came dressed in rich mantles. It was early in the morning when this happened, and we were all ready to start; but Cortés ordered us to wait in our quarters until he could see what was the matter. . . . As soon as the speech-making was over, we at once set out; . . . and since many people came to see us from the neighbouring towns, all the roads were full of them.

'The next day in the morning we reached the great causeway, and continued our march towards Iztapalapa. And when we saw so many cities and villages built in the water, and other large towns on dry land, and that straight, level causeway leading towards Mexico, we were amazed and said that it was like the enchantments they tell of in the book of *Amadis*, from the great towers and temples and buildings rising from the water, and all built of solid masonry; and some of our soldiers even asked whether the things that we saw were not a dream.   It is not to be wondered at that I write like this, for there is so much to think upon that I do not know how to describe it, seeing things never heard of or seen before, not even in dreams, as we saw them. . . . And then when we entered the city of Iztapalapa, the appearance of the palaces in which they lodged us! How spacious they were and well-built, of fine stonework and cedar-wood, and the wood of other sweet-scented trees; with great courts and rooms, wonderful to behold, shaded with awnings and hung with cotton cloth. When we had looked thoroughly at all this, we went into the garden, which was so wonderful a thing to see that I could not look too long at the different trees and notice the scent which each one had; and the borders full of flowers, and the many fruit trees and flowering shrubs, and the pool of fresh water. There was another thing worth seeing: that big canoes could come into the garden from the lake through an opening which had been made, without any need for landing; and all of it was polished and shining with many kinds of stone, and pictures on them which gave one much to think about. Then there were birds of many different kinds and breeds which came to the pool. I say again that I stood looking, and thought that in the whole world there could be no other lands discovered like these; for at that time there was no Peru, nor any idea of it. To-day all is overthrown and lost; nothing is left at all. . . .

'Early next morning we left Iztapalapa. . . . We went along our causeway, which is eight paces wide, and goes so straight to the city of Mexico that it did not seem to me to bend at all. But broad as it is, it was so full of people that there was hardly room for them, some going to Mexico and others coming away, and the Indians who had come to see us, so that we were hardly able to pass by the crowds of those that came. And the towers and temple were full of people as well as the canoes from all parts of the lake; and it was not to be wondered at, for they had never seen horses and men like ours. And as we were looking at such wonderful things, we did not know what to say; whether it was real, that which appeared before us; for on one side, on land, there were large towns, and in the lake, ever so many more. And we saw the whole lake crowded with canoes, and on the causeway many bridges at intervals, while in front of us was the great city of Mexico—and we did not amount to 400 soldiers! We followed our causeway; and when we came to where another smaller causeway branched off, going to Coyoacán—another town, where there are buildings like towers, which are their oratories—many chiefs and caciques approached with rich mantles on their shoulders. These mighty caciques had been sent forward to receive us by the great Montezuma; and

when they came before Cortés they welcomed us in
their language, and for a sign of peace they touched
the ground with their hands, and kissed the ground
with the same hand.   Then we halted a good while;
and from there the caciques went on to meet the great
Montezuma, who was approaching in a rich litter,
accompanied by other great lords and caciques. . . .
The great Montezuma got down from his litter, and
those mighty caciques supported him with their arms
beneath a marvellous rich canopy, coloured with green
feathers, with gold and silver embroidery and pearls
hung from a fringe which was wonderful to look
upon. . . . And when Cortés was told that the great
Montezuma was approaching and saw him coming,
he dismounted from his horse; and when he came
near Montezuma, they both at the same time did each
other reverence.'

The labours, dangers, and sufferings of the small
bands of Spanish explorers have often been described.
One of the grimmest in the whole history of discovery
is the adventure of Almagro, one of Pizarro's captains,
on his expedition to Chile:

'Don Diego de Almagro departed on the discovery
of his conquest, with whom went 570 horsemen and
footmen, well provided of all furniture necessary: yea,
there were some citizens who left their houses and
plantations to go with him. . . . Great were the troubles
which Don Diego and his company passed on the
journey towards Chile, as well with hunger and thirst,
as also with encounter of Indians which were mighty
great men of growth.   Also there were in some places
exceeding good archers who were clothed in seal skins.
But the extreme cold did much annoy them, as well as

the bitter, sharp air, as the frost and snow, and also the passage over the mountains which were covered with snow.[1] Where it happened that a captain called Ruy Díaz, who followed Don Diego de Almagro, had many of his men and horses frozen to death, for neither their apparel nor their armour could resist the exceeding sharpness of the air, which did so vehemently penetrate and freeze them. The extremity of this cold was such that at the end of five months, when Don Diego returned toward Cuzco, he found some of his company which had followed outward, frozen to death, standing on their feet leaning upon the rocks, and holding their horse bridles in their hands; and their horses likewise frozen to death, as fresh without corruption, as though at that instant they had died. The carcasses of which horses was a great relief for his men, at his said return, for want of other victuals. . . .'

Yet success, when it came, was definite and decided:

'Captain Soto was the son of a squire of Jerez, near Badajoz. He went into the Spanish Indies when Peter Arias [Pedrarias] of Avila was governor of the West Indies. And there he was without anything of his own, save his sword and target: and for his good qualities and valour Peter Arias made him captain of a troop of horsemen, and by his commandment he went with Fernando Pizarro to the conquest of Peru . . . whereby in time he gathered an hundred and fourscore thousand ducats together, with that which fell to his part, which he brought into Spain; whereof the Emperor borrowed a certain part, which he repaid

[1] Another account says that the Indian guides took Almagro and his company that way so that they should all die of cold (*Purchas his Pilgrims*, xvii. 276).

again with sixty thousand reals of plate in the rent of
the silks of Granada, and all the rest was delivered
him in the Contractation House of Seville. . . . And
although Soto of his own nature was not liberal, yet
because that was the first time that he was to show
himself in the Court, he spent frankly, and went
accompanied with those which I have named, and with
his servants, and many other which resorted unto him.
He married with Doña Isabel de Bobadilla, daughter
of Pedrarias de Avila, Count of Puñonrostro. The
Emperor made him governor of the Isle of Cuba, and
Adelantado or President of Florida, with a title of
Marquis of certain part of the lands that he should
conquer.'

Besides their sufferings and their success, the *conquistadores* have, even more frequently, been taxed with
acts of cruelty and treachery. These were sometimes
due to fear, or to righteous indignation. Alvarado, in
the absence of Cortés, massacred the unarmed dancers
at a Mexican festival; Nuñez de Balboa, discoverer of
the Pacific, set his dogs on natives suspected of un-
natural vice, and had them torn in pieces. Examples
are too numerous to mention. Yet the Spaniards,
though well armed, were always in an exiguous
minority; and, as crusaders, they felt bound to preach
a standard of morality to others, however badly they
might behave themselves. To an Indian, a Christian
seemed to be a man whose main desires were brown
women and yellow metal. The least excusable of all,
perhaps, is Fernando Pizarro, the conqueror of Peru.
Treachery to his companions was followed by treachery
to the Inca ruler, who was promised his life if he filled
a large room with gold as high as a man could reach

with his sword. He did so, making his captors rich men, but was murdered in spite of it; and it seemed to Garcilaso el Inca, the Spanish-Peruvian author of the

Inca Royal Commentaries, something like divine justice that Pizarro, his brothers, and most of those who were involved in the murder of the Inca Atahualpa, should end their days in civil war, murder, or execution. Pizarro was not only brutal; he was foolish. As long

as he held the Inca emperor a prisoner, he could have ruled the whole Peruvian empire in his name. But the Peruvian state was not a thing which could have been readily understood by an average sixteenth-century European. It has been described as a carefully organized State-socialism, in which value was estimated on the basis of production and was entirely unconnected with the possession of gold.

It needed men like More, Bacon, and Montaigne to realize that the New World held a message for the Old, and that Inca civilization could be described as Utopian in the best sense, before that word had become (as it has become to-day) a term of abuse. Spanish writers in the sixteenth century had heard of Plato's lost island of Atlantis, believed to have sunk beneath the western ocean, and identified it with the newly discovered continent; but they did not see that the Inca polity was comparable in some curious respects to the ideal city which Plato described in his *Republic*. More and Bacon realized that an ideal republic could only exist in a new world, free from all medieval theorizing about Church and State. Vasco de Quiroga, who was sent out as a colonial judge, took with him to Mexico a copy of More's *Utopia*, and regarded it as a text-book on the government of native races: the laws and customs of the Utopians were clearly in his mind when he drew up his *Ordenanzas* for the practical organization and welfare of the Tarascan Indians of Michoacán. He had, like his contemporaries in the University of Salamanca, a profound sense of the value of law as one of the greatest things in the life and achievements of mankind; and he added to it a kindliness and a love for his fellow-men which rank him with the priest Las Casas as one of the great 'apostles to the Indies', and one of the most devoted social workers Spain ever sent to America. Padre de Las Casas was a noble champion of the rights of the American Indians, though his violent venerable figure and his passionate unreason did little practical good to their cause, and much harm to the reputation of Spain. His works were translated into the principal languages of Europe, and he did more than anyone else—except William of Orange—to establish the 'Black Legend' of Spanish cruelty and bigotry, and to prejudice people's minds against Spanish imperialism. Englishmen read his controversy with the lawyer Sepúlveda in Hakluyt's translation: *The sum of the disputation between Fryer Bartholomew de Las Casas and Doctor Sepúlveda*, published in *Purchas his Pilgrims*. Las Casas could never admit, as Sepúlveda did, that there could be just causes for making war on the Indians. The other Spanish exponents of international law tended to agree with Las Casas. Some of them questioned the right of the Spaniards to be in the Indies at all, or took the view that Spain's position was that of a trustee for the Indians' welfare—a conception not unlike the modern mandate under the League of Nations, except that the Spaniards felt themselves responsible not to a League but to the Church. There was, in fact, a striking contrast between the brutalities of the men who made the Empire in America and the profound sense of trusteeship shown by the jurists in the universities in Spain.

Spanish unity under Ferdinand and Isabel had implied the cultural hegemony of Castile. Castilian was the dominant language, and Isabel, the dominant partner in the joint monarchy, was thoroughly Castilian herself. But Charles V, her grandson, was an Austrian. His mother was Juana *la loca* ('Crazy Jane'), daughter of Ferdinand and Isabel; his father was Philip the Fair, Duke of Burgundy, and a Hapsburg. That family was justly proud of its importance in central Europe; but it was quite unable to appreciate the mind of medieval or Renascence Spain. The extravagant Burgundian nobles who accompanied Philip the Fair and the youthful Charles V were typical, uncomprehending tourists in Spain, among the upright, secretive Castilian peasants and the alert, distrustful townsmen.

The Spanish view of Charles differed from the view held in central Europe. That he was a Hapsburg meant nothing to members of the Cortes of Castile. They had probably never heard the name and could certainly never pronounce it; and when, through heavy bribes (for which they themselves had eventually to find the money), Charles was elected Holy Roman Emperor, they thought that he should have consulted the Cortes first, before involving Castile in such immense political and financial commitments. Castile had suffered from that once before, when Alfonso the Sage had been a candidate for the Imperial Crown, and had bribed the electors heavily, but without success. Charles V, when he first came to Spain, was very young and spoke no Spanish. His Flemish advisers formed a barrier between him and the Spanish nobles and prelates, while they distributed the most lucrative administrative posts amongst themselves. The appointment of the twenty-year-old Guillaume de Croy as Archbishop of Toledo was the most glaring

example. In his favour it might be said that he was
a pupil of the great Spanish humanist, Luis Vives, and
that already (at the age of eighteen) he had been Bishop
of Cambrai; but he held the primacy of Spain for two
years without once setting foot in the country.

To the evil of absentee prelates and landlords was
added the evil of an absentee king. While Charles
poured out Spanish wealth in foreign campaigns, he
made the name of Spain famous through three con-
tinents. In the midst of all this brilliant adventure, in
the morning of its Empire and on the threshold of its
European hegemony, with Mexican gold in its ships
and Italian poetry in its ears, the nation was war-
weary. The greatest poet of the age, one of Spain's
finest soldiers, let slip a few lines which sound curiously
modern in their pessimism, their sick horror of the
endless violence, upheaval, and ruined lives. They
come in the first Elegy, written in 1535, a year before
Garcilaso de la Vega was killed fighting in Provence at
the age of thirty-three.

And now, larger than ever lies the curse
 On this our time; and all that went before
Keeps altering its face from bad to worse;

 And each of us has felt the touch of war—
War after war, and exile, dangers, fear—
 And each of us is weary to the core

Of seeing his own blood along a spear
 And being alive because it missed its aim.
Some folks have lost their goods and all their gear.

 And everything is gone, even the name
Of house and home and wife and memory.
 And what's the use of it? A little fame?

The nation's thanks? A place in history?
One day they'll write a book, and then we'll see.

There were other causes of resentment: levies, taxes, and overriding the *fueros*. Charles made a Walloon president of his first Cortes (Valladolid, 1518). The member for Burgos protested, as did many others, demanding more respect for the law of the land. The Flemings were expelled from the chamber, and members reminded the king that it was illegal to give such important posts to foreigners. They begged him to learn Castilian, so that he might understand his subjects better and be understood by them too. The Cortes of Aragon, assembled at Saragossa, put difficulties in the way of his recognition by that part of the joint kingdom. The Cortes of Castile which he summoned to meet at Santiago—a long and expensive journey for all who attended—refused to vote a subsidy for Charles's coronation as Emperor. Toledo, still furious at its Flemish boy-archbishop, sent no properly accredited *procuradores*, but only messengers, or observers. Other *procuradores* refused to take the oath until their protests were heard. They had good ground for protest. The king's foreign favourites were not only in illegal possession of high offices of state: they were proposing to levy illegal taxes. They had also withdrawn from circulation all the gold ducats with the heads of Ferdinand and Isabel and were sending them out of the country, and finally they had, without warning, raised the rents of all Crown lands, a measure which had thrown the whole country into confusion. Bishops protested; preachers inveighed against the new king. Juan de Padilla, a Toledan gentleman who held a municipal appointment (*regidor*), appeared like a John Hampden, as leader of the protest of the Commons.

The king, however, was anxious to be off. He could not understand why those good gentlemen and solemn burgesses were worrying over insignificant details, when he was about to be crowned Emperor of all Christendom. Cortes were instructed to meet him once more, at Corunna. Recalcitrant members were bluntly asked to name their price: what would they take to be quiet?—but those who did so did not long survive their return to their constituencies. The observers from Toledo growled that if Charles left Spain he should set up a regency in which the towns were properly represented. But in the end the king got his grant of money, leaving as regent his former tutor, whom he had made a Cardinal.

These events led straight to the Revolt of the *Comuneros*, members of the discontented *comunidades* or Boroughs of Castile, supported at first by many of the nobles. The movement, if it had succeeded, might ultimately have established a real, effective parliamentary system in Spain, and might have turned the absolute monarchy into a constitutional one. It began in Toledo and Segovia, and spread to some of the oldest and most respected towns in Castile: Zamora, Toro, Burgos, Guadalajara, Soria, Avila, Valladolid, León, and Madrid (then little more than a straggling village). A Council of the Boroughs was held at Avila, and detailed instructions were given by the municipalities to their elected *procuradores*. These instructions show us what the programme of the *Comuneros* was. Some of it was not very new: they wanted to put a stop to misgovernment by the king's foreign favourites and their misuse of public funds, and they agreed that the root of the trouble was the new king's failure to continue with the policy and reforms of Ferdinand and Isabel. This is interesting, because it shows that the townspeople had noticed the difference between the purely Spanish government of the Catholic Sovereigns and what had been happening under the alien rule of Philip the Fair and Charles V.

But the *Comuneros* also had something fresh to demand, about the political and parliamentary representation of the boroughs. They asked that every town should in future send to the Cortes two elected *procuradores*, one from the class of *hidalgos*, or gentlemen, and one from the people. Hitherto some towns had had two *procuradores*, who were both *hidalgos* as a rule, while some had been represented only by one *corregidor* who was not elected but appointed by the king. The new programme would have enforced the election of representatives, and it would also have ensured that the people as well as the gentry should have their own members of parliament. It seems a most modest demand nowadays, but in the early sixteenth century it was much too revolutionary for a Hapsburg king.

Charles V, in order to gain time, persuaded some well-meaning nobles to mediate. The tragedy of the *Comuneros* became the tragedy of all reformist movements in Spain: ambition, muddle, delay, lack of unity, the treachery of an aristocratic supporter on the one hand, and a drift towards extremist violence on the other. The revolt eventually stuck, and refused to go either forward or back. It would have needed a Cromwell or a Bolívar to have led the Boroughs of Castile to victory against Charles V. The leaders they had were men of courage and devotion, who gave their lives for their ideals; but the great leader whom they deserved was not forthcoming, and the movement ended in defeat, like the Republics of 1873 and 1931–39. The Bishop of Zamora raised a force of 1500 men who gave a good account of themselves; but Juan de Padilla, in command of the *Comunero* forces, was caught at a disadvantage at Villalar, defeated, and executed the next morning with his officers and friends. His wife, María Pacheco, gallantly refused to give in, and defended Toledo to the last.

Charles V was a more generous prince than most of his contemporaries. On his return to Spain, after the revolt of the *Comuneros* had been crushed, he granted a belated amnesty and satisfied the least important of their aspirations, giving to Spaniards the offices and employments formerly granted to Flemings. He may have realized that these two excellent peoples were incompatible, and that neither would ever stand being governed by the other.

The lessons of Flemish painting, Flemish weaving, and Flemish counterpoint were valuable in Spain, and the Low Countries profited by sixteenth-century Spanish literature, besides printing quantities of Spanish books. But Charles's son, Philip II, disliked most things Flemish. This was perhaps part of his pose as the typical Spaniard—an attitude which has deceived generations of historians and even Spaniards themselves. But Spaniards are not like that. Philip was Spanish neither in his vices, which were mean and petty, alien to the Spanish temperament and to the Renascence, nor in his virtues, which were those of a German civil servant. Trying to look more Spanish than the Spaniards themselves, he in fact developed a remote, exotic officialdom, rigidly centralized and further than ever out of touch with the Spanish people.

Philip II began work at the age of sixteen, in his father's absence, as a member of the Council of Castile. Charles V wrote detailed instructions for Philip, much as Cardinal Ximénez had written directions for Charles himself; and every day, after the Council had risen, Philip wrote to his father an account of the business done: a report filled with acute observations, and, not least, observations on the economic difficulties with which Spain was beginning to be overwhelmed. He worked like this, without haste and without interruption, for over forty years, keeping everyone waiting until he was ready, perfecting the organization of the State in all its branches. He controlled, personally, every action taken by his agents in every part of the world. Personal initiative was sternly discouraged. The system might have worked with twentieth-century means of communication: long-distance telephone, broadcasting, television, air mail. As it was, news of the rise and fall of prices—or of peoples—took a fortnight to reach him even from Flanders, and six months or a year from the Spanish possessions in America. Philip read and minuted every paper himself. Decisions were delayed. Local conditions had often changed before the instructions from the Escurial were received. Spain achieved world dominion, but its arteries began to harden. As the Crown appointed men who should have been elected by the people, and offices were sold for a fee, the Cortes decayed and the towns lost their interest in local government; though it is true that all this did not pass without criticism.

Throughout the sixteenth century there was much complaint about the defects of the administration and its monetary policy, and people also argued about the nature and rights of kingship. They discussed, for instance, what was the difference between an absolute monarch and a tyrant; and the Jesuit historian Mariana, in a beautifully written Latin dialogue, considered whether in any circumstances it was lawful to kill a king. He decided that it was; but, with an odd squeamishness about the shedding of royal blood, he recommended poison rather than cold steel. His book *De Rege* was publicly burnt in Paris, but it was eagerly consulted by the revolutionaries of England.

Philip was an absolute monarch, but not a tyrant, except perhaps to those who had personal dealings with him. He was rather the minutely conscientious bureaucrat doing his best to check corruption and extravagance. But personal bureaucracy on so vast a scale was beyond any man's powers. There was much to be said for his policy of centralization; local separatist feeling was often inconvenient and sometimes suicidal; the people of Aragon could not possibly be allowed to refuse admission (as they tried to do) to Castilian troops sent for the purpose of defending the Aragonese frontier against France. But the trouble was that centralization did not stop within reasonable limits, and it tended more and more to mean the dominance of Castile over the other peoples of Spain—a dominance which in the seventeenth century darkened into oppression. The Spanish monarchy seems to have had little sense of the distinction—which Rome understood very well—between matters suitable for central control and matters best left to local government. It mistook administrative uniformity for political unity. Had its methods been more elastic, Spain might have become united, not only in the formal sense but in the will and consent of all its peoples. As it was, centralism only aggravated their consciousness of difference, and provoked separatist feeling instead of dissolving it.

More than to any other single cause, the political decay of Spain was due to the failure to create joint Spanish Cortes for the whole country, with representatives from Catalonia, Aragon, the Basque provinces, and all the other regions. Such Cortes would have been able to stand up to the power of the king, and would have preserved the political vitality of the Spanish people. As it was, by the time that Spain acquired a national parliament (the Cortes of Cadiz, 1809), the great medieval Spanish tradition of representative government was dead, or lived on only in village councils.

In the same way as he exaggerated administrative uniformity, Philip pushed to extreme limits his theories of ideological orthodoxy. He declared that it would be better not to reign at all than reign over heretics; and in Spain he was able to suppress opinions that circulated freely in every other part of Europe. He thus prepared the way for that intellectual isolation of Spain which had such disastrous effects on its later development. One of his first cares was the punishment of religious reformers. His reign began with a large and disgusting *auto de fe* (ceremonial execution of heretics) at his capital, Valladolid, where numerous victims were burnt alive for their theological opinions, and not merely burnt in effigy, or strangled first, as some apologists of the Inquisition would have us believe. This barbarous human sacrifice has been condoned on the ground that it prevented the extension to Spain of the wars of religion; but the alternative was a paralysing acquiescence in political and religious censorship of ideas. With the banning to Spanish students of foreign and non-Catholic universities, Spain was automatically cut off from the newer currents of European thought—particularly in science and philosophy—and the good or useful work that was done tended to appear under the mask of religious studies; Ambrosio Morales, for instance, achieved a wonderful survey of Spanish antiquities, while officially occupied in a search for the skull of St. Lawrence, which Philip II wanted to put in his new monastery of the Escurial.

The episode of Philip's journey to England and marriage to Mary Tudor was one of the many expansive schemes of Spanish policy, in which the Church, the Inquisition, and the monarch's private life were merely instruments. In some of the English towns through which he passed Philip thought the entertainment too lavish. There was too much feasting; too much music. The English did not realize, he said, that he was not going to a festival but to a crusade. What he meant was that, through his marriage to Queen Mary, he hoped to bring England within the Spanish sphere of influence. There was to be an English return to Catholicism. Philip won the first round, but the return of England to Catholicism was prevented, and Philip's plans upset, by the imprudence of Queen Mary herself, in her relentless persecution of Protestants. Even Philip tried to restrain Mary in her pious orgies of persecution. Archbishop Carranza, Primate of

Spain, who had himself been persecuted by the Inquisition by reason of his admiration for Erasmus, lifted up his aged voice in favour of toleration in England. But there followed the beheading of Lady Jane Grey, the burning of the four bishops at Oxford: the lighting of the candle which should never be put out. Tolerance at that time was as rare in England as in Spain. The situation was too dangerous. English people could not tolerate a great Spanish king bent on a political hegemony of Europe. Every Catholic in England was suspected—if not always with good reason—of being on the side of Spain; and Philip, if the Invincible Armada had been successful enough to allow him to land troops, would have found a 'fifth column' of Catholics waiting to receive him, and a sufficient number of Englishmen ready to act as quislings. Neither Spanish propaganda nor Spanish gold had been idle; it is well known that there were men in high places in England who were in Philip's pay. But the idea of anglicanism won: the idea of a national, reformed Church in a national State. Yet this was not very different in principle from the idea of Philip II for Spain: a national, Catholic Church which should be an instrument in the world-policy of the Spanish kings.

England had a certain literary interest for many of the Spaniards who accompanied Philip, because it was the scene of Arthurian romance—the background of some of those Books of Chivalry which were afterwards found in the library of Don Quixote. Riding through the wet, green water-meadows between Southampton and Winchester, they caught an occasional glimpse of a farm-hand on an old horse, who must have been—and therefore *was*, as Cervantes would have told it—Urganda la Desconocida, or some other Arthurian damsel on her milk-white palfrey.

Philip also tried to subdue a revolt in the Low Countries, which belonged to the Hapsburg kings of Spain as dukes of Burgundy. But in Flanders the Spaniards found no romantic interest whatever. They could never keep warm; and the unpleasant tasks which they carried out so thoroughly at the orders of the Duke of Alba were a duty best done and forgotten. The Spanish proverbial phrase, 'trailing a pike in Flanders', brings with it the hopelessness and despair of defending a lost cause in a flat, waterlogged country —a cause which was never really theirs, but only their king's. 'We'll never take it, and it's always raining.'

That, perhaps, is why the Spanish infantry never sang in Flanders. But the Dutch did. The greatest Dutch songs, with their fine French, English, Flemish, and German tunes, belong to the time of the Spanish occupation. The Dutch National Anthem is a French tune turned against the Spaniards; other songs cover the Spanish soldiers, and their commanders, with ridicule. Ridicule was one of the great weapons with which the Dutch succeeded in driving the Spaniards out. The very name, *Duque de Alba*, has become a Dutch word, *dukdalf*: the mooring-post to which a Dutch bargee ties up at night.

Flanders, then, left no impression on the Spanish mind beyond a grim duty done, and a word for 'red tape': *balduque*, from the name of the Dutch town Bois-le-duc. There are no great Spanish plays on the subject. When the comic servant is asked what the country is like, he describes a Flemish painting,

but adds that even the stars twinkle because they are
cold.   There is hardly a poem or a ballad; and no
contemporary Spanish history of the Dutch wars
is famous or memorable.   One picture remains:
Velázquez' *Surrender of Breda*; otherwise Flanders is
completely forgotten.

Yet the Spanish occupation of the Netherlands
produced for Philip an adversary worthy of him:
William of Orange.   He had to be put out of the way,
of course—in the manner recommended by the author
of *Utopia* for getting rid of the head of an enemy state:
by assassination.   He was murdered at Delft (1584) by
a fanatical Catholic who believed that he was helping
the Spanish cause.   But William bequeathed to his
countrymen a legacy which the Spaniards were unable
to suppress, a legacy of hate, reprisals, and scorn.   His
views were expressed in an *Apology* (written by a
Frenchman at his orders) refuting the false accusations
contained in the edict of banishment issued against
him by the king of Spain.   It was not political criticism,
but scurrilous personal abuse, comparing Philip's
private life with that of Jupiter.   That was hardly a
true likeness of His Catholic Majesty; but the pamphlet
had a lasting influence on the reputation of Spain
in northern Europe.   Philip II became known as
the supreme example of bigotry and oppression,
while the charges concerning his private life gained
credence a few years later through the memoirs of his
former secretary, Antonio Pérez.   Only one thing can
make Philip seem human to us now: Verdi's music in
the opera *Don Carlos*.

Philip died in his modest apartment in the Escurial
—the immense monastery he had built in the mountains

near Madrid, the office from which he had ruled an empire. From the window of his workroom he could look down on the majestic landscape of New Castile stretching away in tranquil, austere beauty to the plains of La Mancha. He had his devotional books, his little Flemish pictures, the chamber-organ on which one of his daughters had played to him. As he lay in bed he could see, through another window, the priests saying Mass at the high altar of the monastery church; they were so close that he could hear the swish of their vestments as they made the ritual movements, or correct an inexperienced server who stood in the wrong place. Had it been in vain, that lifetime of devotion to his country and his God? Surely he had been cheated by the winds and waves, not by Elizabeth of England; by the principle of evil, not by William of Orange; by blind economic forces, not by Genoese bankers? He died, his body covered with relics and lice, his mind obsessed by the inviolable purity of dogma and the thought of life beyond the grave; to some of his subjects, in glory; to others, in remoteness and suspicion. The Spain that he had made was the Spain of Cervantes, and of *Don Quixote*.

CHAPTER V

THE SPAIN OF CERVANTES

THE Spain of *Don Quixote* seems a typical land of the Renascence. Yet the outlook and habits which persisted in it, long after the Renascence had begun in Italy, were in some ways medieval. Spanish builders, like their fellows in England, went on building a sort of Gothic far into the sixteenth century. Earlier, at a time when the liveliest Spanish inspiration was Moslem, most of the true Gothic cathedrals had been designed by French or German architects—except in Catalonia, which shared the tradition of southern France. Then, tardily and anachronistically, Spaniards adopted the foreign Gothic style and turned it into a thing of their own, combining its principles with the broad aisles and flattened arches of the cathedral of Plasencia, or with the box-like construction of Segovia and its expanse of rose-pink walls. Spanish 'Gothic' is really a Renascence afterthought.

By the time of *Don Quixote*, indeed, this architecture was old-fashioned, and was being superseded by the new Graeco-Roman buildings which expressed the intelligent splendour of an imperial court. But in literature, one medieval form was still exploding by delayed action. The date and origin of Spanish ballads is much disputed; what is certain, however, is that the popular ballad-forms, which in the early fifteenth century were avoided by educated writers, afterwards came into their own, and swept like a wind through the literary circles of Spain. Not only did fashionable poets write ballads of chivalry—and they are first-rate poems, not academic exercises—but playwrights adapted the ballad verse-form to lyrical and dramatic purposes, so that it became an even handier instrument of Spanish poetry than blank verse is of English. For a Latin language this was a stroke of technical genius. The ballad, or *romance*, uses short lines which restrain any temptation to be pompous or bombastic; it also uses assonant vowels instead of perfect rhymes, and this saves Spanish verse from the banal effects of rhyme in a tongue where rhyming is too easy to be charming to the ear. Above all, poetry was kept within speaking distance of the people, and away from the artificial, scholastic tendencies of French and Italian versification.

Naturally, the *romances* written in Cervantes' day by Góngora or Lope de Vega were not like the early popular ballads. But the point is that they were still ballads and yet they were modern lyrics, all new and hot. In such an atmosphere the books of chivalry which Cervantes parodied seemed more modern than they did elsewhere. Their sham-antique language (which Malory and Spenser also used) was a convention much like the tough American lingo of a gangster film. *Don Quixote* is not only a satire but also the last and greatest of all Books of Chivalry, told by Cervantes in his ordinary voice, which is a voice of the Renascence.

The personality of the Spanish people did not consist only of quixotism or the spirit of a crusade, nor of those qualities (mostly the results of later misgovernment) which non-Spanish writers have made part of the *leyenda negra*, the Black Legend: religiosity, cruelty, unpunctuality. The Black Legend has been baked too black, abroad; in Spain, its features were more often and more sharply criticized than is commonly supposed. There were undoubtedly mental reserves in all classes of the population: things which it was dangerous to express in public or even in private; but there were also things which most people in Spain approved, tolerated, or accepted. Certain ideas in sixteenth-century Spain seemed not so much doctrines as ways of thinking that were inevitable. People did not regard them merely as correct opinions; these were ideas which had become so much part of their minds that they never thought of them at all. They did not see them: they saw other things through them. There was the religious ideal, for instance. It may have been exaggerated or misunderstood, but it was certainly a repeated note all through Spanish life, though it was only one form, one expression, of a spiritual need with which Spanish minds were always preoccupied. In Spain there were very few who were anti-religious or anti-Catholic, though there have always been Spaniards in all ages who have been anti-clerical.

Castilians in the days of Ferdinand and Isabel had quick and supple minds, attracted by all forms of intellectual curiosity, by adventures of the spirit as well as by adventures of travel and exploration. As the century drew on, there came not only soldiers and explorers but colonial administrators and international lawyers, writers of fine poetry and superb prose, originators, also, of bold political thought. The characters of literature were of the people, rather than of the court; indeed the court was not a fixed institution, but nomadic: Ferdinand and Isabel, jointly or singly, moved about the country with an establishment like an army headquarters, setting up their standard first in one small country town and then in another. The *Celestina*, the great early Spanish novel in dialogue (which was afterwards translated into many languages and went the round of Europe), takes place in a small town in Castile. It might be Salamanca or Toledo, though there is no mention of a university or a cathedral, nor indeed of any public institutions or public men, except for a scandalous joke about the French Ambassador; only an enamoured youth, a girl with well-to-do parents, an underworld of night-life, and the Spanish Bawd herself, talking and talking as nobody talked again until *Don Quixote* and *The Merry Wives of Windsor*.

The Catalans, now, were looking towards Castile. They had had a good medieval literature, but in Renascence times their chief contribution to the library of the Peninsula was made by a poet who wrote in Castilian and conveyed to Castile the forms of the new Italian writing. Juan Boscán translated the immortal Italian dialogue of Baldassare Castiglione, *The Courtier*, and in doing so invented a new and wonderful literary instrument: Renascence Castilian prose. Boscán may have been himself only a minor poet, but he was the friend and inspirer of Garcilaso de la Vega. It was Boscán who (in his own words) 'said to himself, why not try in the Castilian language the sonnets and other lyric forms used by the best authors in Italy?' It was Garcilaso who handled these forms in his irresistible Spanish style; whose poems were printed in small duodecimo editions in Antwerp, Rome, Venice, Naples, and Paris, were carried to the ends of the earth in the pockets of Spanish soldiers, and influenced every great literature in Europe.

Garcilaso was also a favourite Spanish poet for setting to music. The composers for *vihuela* (the Spanish lute, shaped and tuned not unlike a modern guitar) made songs from his sonnets; and later in the century his poems were used as words for madrigals. By that time, his imagery seemed too pagan, and the verses were slightly emended to give them a mystical or devotional character—divine parodies, they were called. Spanish music was flourishing at this time as a cultivated art, as well as a popular diversion and a handmaid of religion. Germaine de Foix, a descendant of the Cid and the widow of Ferdinand the Catholic by his second marriage, held a salon in Valencia at which Luis Milán, a famous virtuoso, played his compositions and accompanied his settings of old Spanish ballads. What really interested Milán was the practice and performance of music as a necessary part of all social intercourse. He wrote a book of parlour games and a guide to polite behaviour, *El Cortesano*, which was one of the many descendants of Castiglione's work. He insists on the value of sprightly conversation; his characters are the great-uncles and great-aunts of the men and women of seventeenth-century English comedy, of Wycherley and Congreve. Milán delights in sentimental complications, but he is clever enough to make passion a little ridiculous: for instance, in the situation of a lover who is bidden to attend his lady in the chicken-house. Besides this polite music of the court, there were popular tunes collected by Francisco Salinas, professor of music in the university of Salamanca. He was blind from birth, and his memories of Spain (and of Rome, where he had studied) were all musical—tunes he had heard people singing in the streets. His playing on one of the little pedal-less organs of the period inspired his friend, Luis de León, to his greatest poem.

Luis de León was equal in genius to Garcilaso, but a man of a very different character. He was an Augustinian monk, a Christian whose faith was too deeply penetrated with thought to be altogether safe in the orthodoxy of his time. He was suspect to the Inquisition, and was imprisoned for five years until the case against him was withdrawn. The charge was mainly due to a colleague at the university of Salamanca; and his knowledge of Hebrew and interest in the language led to the suspicion that he might have Jewish ancestry. The intellectual equipment of Luis de León resembled that of Milton; it included Hebrew as well as Greek and Latin. In that sense he was a fine example of the scholarly poet of the Renascence. But Spain lived its Renascence in its own way, not only as a great awakening of the spirit but also as 'a rebirth of conscience in search of the light'. Luis de León was untiring in his search. He knew the material world only too well; he was hurt by it. But he was not overcome; he neither accepted it nor idealized it. His vision began in profound disillusionment. He fled from the misguided majority: the world of lost labour, false peace, undeserved evil. His first escape was to the peace of the country, as it was with the Roman poet Horace, whose verse he imitated; but this was only a temporary stage. His permanent refuge was music, which he found to be a place of clarity, a revelation of truth, and an explanation of the universe. But Luis de León had also read Plato; for him heaven was the place of ideas and pure thought, and his ideal world—

the world of his greatest poetry—is one in which the Christian faith and Platonic clarity formed a whole. Heaven was not only supreme music; it was seeing and understanding: supreme light and supreme intelligence. He hoped for heaven, not as a rest from his labours but to see the essential principle of all things. His flight was not an escape, but a search.

Luis de León was not a mystic in the ordinary sense, or even in the sense in which the word is loosely applied by writers on Spain to almost any devotional writer. Like Milton, he achieved his mystic vision by means of music. His manuscripts show that writing verse was an intellectual agony. His contemporary, Juan de la Cruz, on the other hand, had a fluency which would have been fatal to a less inspired writer. If Garcilaso, in the manner of his inspiration, is the Mozart of Spanish poets, Luis de León is the Beethoven and Juan de la Cruz the Gounod. He has a natural gift of melody; and although, compared with Luis de León, he has little to say, he knows how to make exquisite use of imagery derived from the Song of Songs and of ideas from Plotinus.

Santa Teresa, the greatest of the Spanish devotional writers, had plenty to say of her own, and the gift of writing exactly as she spoke. One can hear her excited, compelling voice as she describes her life and her spiritual experiences; and her voice is inimitable. The Lord was just as likely to be found among the pots and pans in the kitchen as in a convent cell or a cloud of incense. Teresa had the energy and the formidable organizing power of her own age: those qualities which Ignatius Loyola showed in creating the Society of Jesus, and which the Jesuits in their turn displayed in planning vast new territories of America. Yet, unlike Ignatius, she belongs to the religious tradition of the Middle Ages: her faith was secure but not narrow, passionate without losing its humanity and common sense. She was not learned, but she was not out of place in a time when men of letters were alert and open-minded, aware of all that was going on around them in prose and poetry, in scholarship, in politics and thought. In spite of the Inquisition (which was not quite happy about Santa Teresa, either) it was still possible to discuss things openly, and humanists were enjoying the ideal beauties of Italian culture: Garcilaso's poetic paganism, or the platonism of Castiglione or of León Ebreo, which appears in Cervantes' pastoral and Arcadian novel *La Galatea*.

Along with these Italian, pagan, and classical influences there had been currents from the North. They had come in, apparently, with those supercilious feudal aristocrats in the suite of Philip the Fair and Charles V: a first breath of the Reformation. This did not result in anything so un-Spanish as Luther; it filtered through finer minds, in which an inquiring, Hellenizing soul was joined to a tougher, rebellious will. That was the type of Spanish mind which felt the influence of the great scholar and reformer Erasmus; indeed the effect of his ideas in Spain in the time of Charles V was to produce a wave of spiritual fervour which might have led to a religious revolution, and a Spain with a reformed church of its own—not Lutheran, but of a new, more tolerant Spanish pattern—might have become one of the leaders of reformed Europe, instead of a home for the counter-reformation. Erasmus showed Spaniards the prospect of a religion full of mental enthusiasm, but with a scorn for public prostrations, fasts, and pilgrimages—for all those things which, in England and New England, were to be known as Popish practices. He had influential supporters; his admirers included two archbishops, one of whom was Inquisitor-General. They were a minority, of course, the first of that succession of cultivated minorities which have had such noticeable influence in Spain : earnest, civilized men (like the followers of Don Francisco Giner in the nineteenth and early twentieth centuries), devoted and enthusiastic, untiring in the cause of honesty, clear thought, and education.

There was more in the thought of Erasmus to appeal to Spaniards than criticism of religious practices. There was something which Professor Bataillon has called 'Tolstoyan radicalism' in the application of Christian doctrine to human conduct. The Spanish friends of Erasmus saw that the part of religious observance which depended on the Gospels had grown lax; yet that was the only part which, in their opinion, mattered. The teaching of Christ had been adapted to fit the way of the world, they said; and though the Gospels had a clear meaning for every man, by no means every man applied that meaning to himself. The dangerous doctrine that the Gospels meant what they said—or seemed to say—and meant the same for all men, was held by all the Spanish disciples of Erasmus. An illustration of the same liberal attitude is to be found in *Don Quixote*, in the adventure in which the galley-slaves are set free, and in the arguments given in justification of their liberty—although Don Quixote's clear and straightforward reasoning leads him into absurd conclusions.

Alfonso de Valdés, Latin Secretary to the Emperor, thought that every Christian should learn a trade, as was the custom among Moslems and Jews. Monks should not be excepted, nor the sons of gentlemen, nor even of princes. They should be able to make a living by working for it; those who did not work should not eat, he said. The poor, he added, had a right to share in the income of the rich; while the income of the prince was public money, and should not be wasted in imperialistic and religious wars. It is curious to hear such sentiments expressed by a Secretary of Charles V; yet they are to be found in the *Dialogue of Mercury and Charon*, a book which set out to defend the Emperor's policy. Erasmus went further: there are statements in his *Handbook for the Christian Soldier* (who significantly enough appears in Spanish as *caballero cristiano*, Christian knight) which seem to deny the right of property altogether. These passages were toned down by the Spanish translator; but even so they were afterwards condemned by the censorship.

The finest flower of the mind of Erasmus in Spain was not Alfonso de Valdés, but his brother Juan. One of the gentlest and most attractive characters in the whole of Spanish history, he was at once a Renascence scholar and something very like a Quaker, a humanist with the Inner Light. He was a man of two minds, like Cervantes, full of subtle and unobtrusive paradox; a Castilian from Cuenca living by the Bay of Naples, a man born where the austere Castilian landscape looks as if it were made of steel, living in sight of the irresistible beauty and sensuality of Posilipo and Capri—in that 'South Wind' which has rotted the moral fibre of so many men from harsher climates. The fibre of

Juan de Valdés was not rotted. His circle maintained an austerity of conduct and an intellectual honesty unsurpassed in its time. He was a man of two hostile cultures: a mind which paused to consider and to contemplate. This new spirit was not allowed to become naturalized in Spain. The Inquisition saw to that; any Spaniard suspected of reformist ideas (and more particularly if he were partly or wholly of Moslem or Jewish descent) was handed over to the Secular Arm, and that was the end of him, while his property was confiscated to pay the Inquisitor's costs.

A faint flicker of Erasmian wit is still to be detected at the beginning of the seventeenth century in the satire, scepticism, and gentle irony of the author of *Don Quixote*. From his schoolmaster, Lope de Hoyos, Cervantes is thought to have received a smattering of Renascence humanism; but it had to be expressed in an undertone. The peculiarly Erasmian type of humour loved to make a point which would puncture a windy discourse. The temptation to do so was so alive in Cervantes that he even conveyed it to Don Quixote himself. He loved witty sayings and anecdotes with a double meaning and, above all, proverbs (*refranes*), those 'short sentences drawn from long experience' so characteristic of the Spanish genius. More than any other writer of the age of Philip III, he remained faithful to the ideal of transparent simplicity in writing, formulated by Juan de Valdés; and the few modern critics who have cast aspersions on his style have forgotten that they are listening to a speaking voice. The spirit of his works, too, is more human than that of his contemporaries. In place of the savage code of honour ending in bloodshed, so beloved by the

dramatists, Cervantes preferred to show men behaving
in a manner that was more natural and at the same
time more civilized. They may not forgive—God
alone can do that; but they can forget, and they know
that the complicated Spanish code of 'honour' is more
a matter of etiquette than of morals: dishonour does
not appear as dishonour until it is made public, so that
most problems can be solved by keeping one's mouth
shut. That is the ethic of Cervantes' *Exemplary
Novels*.

Cervantes seems to have taken care to conciliate the
orthodox; but he was not (as some have declared) a
hypocrite, nor yet an infidel hiding his secret thought
behind unctuous protestations of religiosity. He was,
on the contrary, an enlightened believer, for whom not
everything in his religion was on the same level of
credibility or importance. He could smile (as the
Erasmists had) at many things held in veneration by
the general public, though the new orthodoxy laid
down by the Council of Trent obliged him to be
prudent and reserved. He even had some inkling of
comparative religion; he knew, for instance, that a
certain festival near Talavera, to which he refers more
than once, was pre-Christian in origin, and that the
object of devotion was a pagan goddess who had
afterwards turned into the Virgin Mary. The shade
of Erasmus appears again when Cervantes smiles
sweetly and rather irreverently at certain ritual acts:
prayers gabbled off by the dozen, miracles, the renown
of certain sanctuaries and places of pilgrimage, covered
with little models of arms and legs dedicated to celebrate
the healing of a wound or disease; Don Quixote, half-
naked, repeating the penance of the legendary Amadis

of Gaul and making a rosary out of the tail of his shirt
—a passage at which the Inquisition took offence. The
complications of Catholic ritual inspired him with only
moderate reverence. He had once lived in the house-
hold of a cardinal; but the ceremony of the *mutatio
capparum*, when the Roman cardinals changed into
their summer vestments, came to his mind when he
was thinking how Sancho changed the saddle of his
ass. It was not a question of insulting or denying the
Catholic faith; Cervantes merely shows the normal and
traditional anti-clericalism of the Spanish people, the
sense of humour which is not necessarily repressed
because religious matters are in question. The few
monks who appear in his writings are all comic; the
two portly Benedictines on their mules as big as
dromedaries, with their sunshades and spectacles, are
in the tradition of medieval Spanish humour.
Cervantes remarks that the hermits of his time were
not like those of early Church history, clothed in palm-
leaves and feeding on roots; the vocation of a hermit
was the very thing for a poor devil who wanted to live
without overwork. The clergy are sometimes treated
with more respect; the Duke's private chaplain is a
figure of ridicule, but the parish priest of Don Quixote's
village is a kindly sympathetic character, and the Canon
of Toledo a learned and enlightened man. But the
character in whom Cervantes seems to have expressed
his ideal of the good life is a layman: the man in the
green cloak, *el caballero del verde gabán*, a pattern of
moderation and wisdom. Such an ideal—lay piety
without ostentation—is evidence of the Erasmist connexions of Cervantes more convincing than all his little
ironies on monks and rosaries. If Spain had not

passed through an Erasmian phase first, we should have had no *Don Quixote*.

It is easy to find ancestors for the novel in Spain: Italian or Alexandrian love-stories, medieval fables, Arthurian romance; and nearer home, in Spain itself, the tragi-comedy in dialogue which begins with *La Celestina*, and the picaresque autobiographical story of a down-and-out, *Lazarillo de Tormes*, by an unknown author of the mid-sixteenth century. *Lazarillo* is one kind of novel: the satirical. What holds the attention is not so much the boy-hero and his feelings as the different sorts of people he meets up and down Spain: the hungry squire, the hot-gospeller selling Papal Bulls, and the most horrible blind man in literature until Pew in *Treasure Island*. But the novel as we know it to-day, with its developing characters, its vision of the world's ways and criticism of life, is the invention of the author of *Don Quixote*—and particularly of the second part of *Don Quixote*.

Cervantes presents the whole Spanish world of his time: not only the picaresque world of thieves and gipsies, but the undergraduates of Salamanca or Bologna, the Duke and Duchess in their country home, the prisoner of war escaped from the Moslems, the ships in port at Barcelona, the state official staying at an inn on his way to embark for America. It is from *Don Quixote* that we can see, better than anywhere else, what people in general thought of that powerful engine of administration, constructed and set going by Ferdinand and Isabel, accelerated by Charles V, complicated and slowed down by Philip II. Magistrates and government officials seemed the natural enemies of the poor and needy; they belonged heart and soul to anyone who bribed them; self-interest was the only motive of their actions. Appointments were only made for a fee, and only accepted in order to get rich quickly. A just judge, a disinterested official, were rare. The administration seemed a mixture of jobbery, corruption, and incapacity. People in general did not so much criticize as accept. Things had always been pretty much like that. Cervantes was not sentimental over the good old days. He never seriously confronted the present with the past, or compared the manners of his own time with the virtues of a golden age. On the contrary he believed that his own times were probably a little better than others. He too had served Philip II, and could not be unaware of certain measures taken to redress wrongs. For Philip had an immense solicitude for his subjects; that is the good side of his method of government. Whenever he had exact information of anything, and time to attend to it, he never hesitated to probe it to the bottom. He was ready to sacrifice the highest dignitary in the state, if he failed him; he valued the humbler officials, and would back them up with all his weight and influence. In Calderón's play, he supports the Mayor of Zalamea, who had executed an army officer for rape. Yet Philip ends, in the play, by upsetting the whole system of a democratically elected office, when he appoints Pedro Crespo mayor of Zalamea for life. That shows how a just and careful government can still be dangerous to liberty.

Some have seen in the description of the Island of Barataria, governed by Sancha Panza, a satire on the administrative system of Spain in the time of Cervantes. It is partly true; but the moral is rather that there was no such thing as the science of being a civil servant: any sensible Sancho could deal with such questions by the light of nature. Don Quixote knew that there was no need for much special knowledge to be governor of an island, though he gave Sancho some memorable advice on the subject; some governors could hardly read or write, although they made lynx-eyed officials.

It has been claimed that Cervantes, as well as satirizing books of chivalry and degenerate forms of chivalrous romance—the nominal reason for writing *Don Quixote* —was also criticizing *hidalguismo*: the idea of the useless, honourable, pitiable, hungry hidalgo (gentleman), the most characteristic product of Spanish social conditions and of the economic consequences of the discovery of America. The anonymous author of *Lazarillo de Tormes* has drawn the poor hidalgo with sure touches, coming out of his house brushing away the crumbs which he would like others to imagine had fallen on his clothes, and picking his teeth to give an impression of the meal which he had not eaten. Cervantes, it is said, killed *hidalguismo* by making his readers laugh gently and kindly at the most sympathetic of all hidalgos. But Don Quixote was not by any means in such a desperate economic condition. He was idle the greater part of the year, certainly; but he had enough to live on, and his table, though modest, was not ill-provided. He was also most careful not to appear with patched clothes or darned stockings—at any rate stockings darned with wool of another colour; and he was seriously put out when one of them laddered at an important moment in his adventures.

Many social and spiritual conditions of the time have been thought to be reflected in *Don Quixote*: Ignatius

Loyola, for instance, founding the new military order of Jesuits for the defence of the Catholic faith against the Reformers. It is possible to take a wider view, and to see Philip II defending the old Spanish order and the old religion—though both were comparatively new, in their Renascence shape. The cause was indeed quixotic, and may have been somewhere at the back of Cervantes' mind when he made his hero go forth into the modern world to restore the lost ideal of chivalry. Was chivalry so very different from the earlier, simpler, pre-tridentine faith which had been insulted and struck in the face by Luther, and only restored—in a sadder and wiser form—by the plastic surgery of the counter-reformation? Was Philip, the paladin of a Universal Church sending the loyal, uncomprehending Spanish infantry through the sodden fields of Flanders, more splendid—or more ridiculous— than Don Quixote leading the loyal uncomprehending Sancho Panza over the scorching plain of La Mancha? But we must beware of allegorical interpretations. Unamuno and other modern critics have given us their own Don Quixotes; we should never forget that the first, most complete, and most convincing commentary on *Don Quixote* is that of his original inventor.

Cervantes also lets us see the beginning of a great Spanish institution: the theatre. I can remember (he says in the introduction to his volume of plays and interludes published in 1615) when all the properties of an actor-manager consisted of a few beards and shepherds' crooks and could be carried in a single sack; while the stage was a platform made from a few boards supported by benches. Two or three musicians sat on the stage itself, in front of a tattered backcloth which opened in the middle to give the characters their exits and their entrances. Some writers have doubted Cervantes' word; but it is fully confirmed by a contemporary print in the British Museum. Cervantes also shows us an amateur performance: a party acting an eclogue of Camoens or Garcilaso out of doors; declaiming fine verses in fine clothes, with such effect as to make Don Quixote decide, if ever he took to the road again, to adopt the life of an Arcadian shepherd and accept the pastoral convention by which men and women, on a basis of sex-equality, took to the hills and vales with a few sheep or goats and occupied themselves in the study of literature, philosophy, and music.

An earlier adventure of Don Quixote concerned a professional company of actors and actresses—women were allowed on the stage in Spain long before they were in England—travelling from one village to the next in their stage costumes, ready to act in a mystery play. But the adventure which sums up the whole of quixotic idealism and absurdity is the adventure of Master Peter's Puppet Show (made into an opera by Falla). The play which the puppets perform shows how Don Gaiferos, a knight at the court of Charlemagne, delivers the Lady Melisendra who has been carried off by the Moslems of Saragossa. Numberless Moors ride out in pursuit; it looks as if the two Christian lovers will be overtaken, and brought back 'tied to their horse's tail, which would be a horrid spectacle'. This is too much for Don Quixote's sense of chivalry. His madness returns; something happens in his mind; the puppets have become real Moors whom a knight-errant is bound to attack. He draws his sword and rushes into the fray; and when the puppet-show is in ruins, and the puppets 'all cut to fitters', he exclaims to the spectators in triumph that now they know what use to the world are knights-errant.

Cervantes himself had tried to be a dramatist; but no manager would risk a new play from an unknown ex-service man out of employment. His plays were, it is true, conceived in an older convention than the plays of Lope de Vega, whom Cervantes despised for playing down to the least intelligent part of the audience, the groundlings or *mosqueteros*. Lope, with his astonishing facility in improvising well-made plays and his fluency in musical and effective verse, turned the course of Spanish drama from the more Elizabethan conception of Cervantes; and the public theatres, which began to open in Madrid, Lima, and Mexico at about the same date as they did in London, were dominated by the operatic manner of Lope de Vega.

Lope's plays have the structure of opera, but not the dramatic vices which have, somehow, in England, come to be associated with it. He scattered his works with some of the most beautiful lyrics in the language: one of them has a refrain of exquisite nonsense which needs no knowledge of Spanish:

> *Piraguamonte, piragua,*
> *Piragua jevizarizagua.*

He could make country people speak as country people do—and behave so as well. In *Peribañez y el Comendador de Ocaña* a wicked gentleman comes to seduce a peasant's young wife one night when her husband is away. She repels him; and next day, when the husband returns, he hears the labourers singing in the fields. They know all about last night's incident: they have made a song about it, and the whole neighbourhood is singing it by then. That is Spain to the life.

In a Spanish town, too, Lope always knows where he is. His staging is precise and vivid: the great Moslem bridge over the Tagus at Toledo, the Guadalquivir at Seville with its white barges and green oars, or the lovely picture of the streets of Madrid in the early morning, when the fountains shoot above the walls of the Duke's garden, and the birds sing fugues, and the dung-carts trundle round clearing the roadways, and the stalls are covered with white milk-bread, and French street-sellers cry 'Marmalade and brandy!'

Marmalade and brandy, butter and fresh rolls, was Góngora's winter breakfast, so he tells us in a poem. The word Gongorism is generally used to mean all that is artificial, involved, and affected in poetic style. In fact, however, many of Góngora's best poems happen to be written in the direct, 'popular' tradition which he and his contemporaries had polished into a form of high art. In some of them he uses dialect or pidgin-Spanish. His sonnets have never been bettered in any literature; he knew inevitably how to rise to the culmination of a sonnet, and when to unwind it to a close. But it is only in the last few years that readers have begun to recapture the beauty of those longer poems in which he worked out the baroque manner that is called Gongoristic. They are not easy to read: the syntax is distorted like the filigree setting of a sapphire, to make a chosen word sparkle (for the great magic of Góngora is in the scintillation of his words); the imagery is coiled into conceits to create a world far from nature, impossible and clear, of sculptured rocks and lacquered sea, a siren land traversed by processions from a frieze of Bernini. Góngora's landscapes are no more natural than a firework display; they are not to be seen anywhere, though under the solid light of a Latin sun they can be dreamed, by people who have forgotten Wordsworth.

Often, in Spain, one comes across a vast church nobly designed on the grandest scale, then left unfinished and ragged, as if some great vision had been broken off. In the course of Spanish history much gigantic effort, and many magnanimous enterprises, have come to a ragged ending. The artists of the sixteenth century were not touched by this malady. Cervantes died in 1616; the drama of Calderón, the painting of Velázquez, the architecture of Churriguera were still to come; the Golden Age was not going silver yet, and there was no apparent failure of nerve or of invention. Yet, in searching for the origins of later defeat, it is tempting to ask these writers whether, even in their own success, they can drop any hint of the fatal cause.

Two universes were present in the Spanish consciousness. Both partook of Christian belief, but one was human and humorous, reaching back to the medieval tradition, while the other was a mystical imperialism of which Spain's earthly empire seemed only the symbol. With its insatiable glory before their eyes, Spaniards grew apt to wonder if anything they had been doing was, after all, worth while; to feel upon all their conquests what T. E. Lawrence called the tarnish of achievement. The Spanish are not a philosophically gifted people; it is in dramatic form that they are sometimes made aware of the two universes coexisting, and the doubt as to which is real. Casandra, the village girl of Gil Vicente's play, believes that she is the Virgin Mary, and tries to make the village believe it too; then, at last, she knows tragically that it was all a mistake. Garcilaso's distracted shepherd thinks his own body has been stolen from him, and sees it lying in a glassy pool. 'Life's a dream,' Calderón declares in his most famous play. *No son todos ruiseñores*, says Góngora; not all these are nightingales, singing between the flowers: it is a music of the mind. 'Didn't I tell you, sir,' says Sancho, 'that they were only windmills?' And at the end of the journey, when Don Quixote is near to disillusion and death, they stop at an inn; and Sancho notices that for the first time his master does not call the inn a castle.

CHAPTER VI

THE HARDENING OF THE ARTERIES

By the middle of the seventeenth century—by the end of the sixteenth even—it was clear that something had gone wrong. Spain (which from 1580 to 1640 included Portugal) was at last a united peninsula: one law, one faith, one sword; under a king who was the first gentleman in Europe, and who ruled an empire, in Europe, Asia, Africa, America, and Oceania, on which the sun never set. Yet if we study the faces of a group of those empire-builders—in El Greco's picture of the *Burial of Count Orgaz*, for instance, with its gathering of neurotic gentlemen in mourning, surrounded by priests and friars—we find a sense of frustration. These men—spare in body and dignified in bearing, with pale faces and black, piercing eyes—are no laughing cavaliers like the Dutch, overflowing with eupeptic satisfaction at being alive, having won their country from Spain and a considerable share in the world's good things, even if (as the Spaniards thought) they had lost their own souls. The men painted by El Greco had also won an enormous share in the world; but its good things, by accident or indifference, had mostly slipped through their fingers. They had not lost their own souls—far from it—nor their very un-Dutch sense of humour, with the reserved twinkle sometimes bursting out into unbridled natural merriment; but they could never really enjoy the world's good things, because each was secluded in his *castillo interior*, the inner castle of his mind. Also, they had never really won their own country. That country was governed on the most up-to-date, centralized system; everything was minutely regulated. Yet it was not well managed, and it had few comforts. There was Italy, for instance: not a nation but a mere geographical expression; and Holland: a collection of heretical provinces built on the mud washed out to sea by a great river. Yet in Italy (as Cervantes knew) there was good food, and in Holland there was abundance; but in Spain, a great national state with a great empire, there was never enough. The men attending the burial of Count Orgaz were not necessarily ascetics or mystics, world-losers or world-forsakers. They simply had not had enough to eat. Or at any rate, they lived in a country which was underfed.

In Spain it is not easy to be wise, even after the event. The famous Decadence has given rise to a considerable literature, both in Spain and in other countries. Much of it is unhistorical, and falsified by the assumption that things were bound to go wrong, and that Spain—from the very nature of the country and the people—was predestined to fail. Actually there are no good grounds for assuming any such thing. Spain had seemed to hold all the cards. The signs of decay, taken singly, were no worse than those that could be observed at different times in other countries, and plenty of Spaniards perceived them before they had gone too far. Though the remedies proposed by mid-seventeenth-century reformers were often useless or absurd, by the eighteenth century the causes of the Spanish failure were beginning to be understood, and intelligent measures taken to meet them. But it has been one of the tragedies of Spanish history that a period of enlightenment and understanding has always

been followed by a period of obscurantism and reaction; and in this case the free inquiry and planning
of Charles III was followed by the ignorance and
credulity of Charles IV.

It is doubtful whether the decadence of a State can
ever be explained simply or completely. As in the
Western Empire of Rome, so in Spain, apparent causes
may be only symptoms or manifestations of a general
breakdown. The symptoms can be described; but
there is no final answer to the question why the arteries
have hardened, what destroyed the power of recovery,
how it was that the new always proved weaker than the
old and the capacity for survival outran the capacity for
replacement. The trouble with Spain was not so
much what happened as what failed to happen, and
what failed to happen can only be described by
comparison or conjecture.

Two of the most complete and impartial accounts
of the decadence—though neither of them answers all
the questions—are those of the English historian,
H. T. Buckle, and the Spanish physiologist, S. Ramón
y Cajal. Both these essays were incidental to other
inquiries. Buckle, in a lengthy introduction to a
history of civilization in England, was examining the
history of Spain 'with the object of elucidating principles on which the history of England supplies
inadequate information'. Cajal was led to his inquiry
through asking himself the question why Spain was so
backward in science. Had Spaniards lost faculties
which they had once possessed? Or were there
disciplines which they had never mastered: for instance,
science? If the second of these were true, there need
be no question of decadence; but it would be necessary

to explain how it was that Spanish people lacked any gift for scientific thinking. Speaking as a scientist, Cajal naturally assumed that the prosperity of nations was largely due to their success in science, and the applications of science to the life and welfare of every citizen. Spaniards however had generally shown a curious incapacity for scientific research. The most obvious explanation was political: the instability of Iberian institutions in modern times had always scattered a group of promising young scientists before they could accomplish anything of permanent value— as it has now scattered the pupils of Cajal himself and of Juan Negrín.

Cajal assessed the output of Spanish scientific work at various periods, including that of the discovery and colonization of America (which had suddenly offered so splendid a field for scientific investigation) and the age of mental prostration which followed the political and economic mistakes of the seventeenth century. His conclusion was that the scientific output of Spain had always remained at approximately the same level, while in comparison with the rest of Europe Spaniards showed poverty in scientific thought and backwardness in invention. They had neglected theory for utility. They did not realize, Cajal stated, that in science only ideas are fertile. In Spain the search for prescriptions and working formulae seemed to have deprived scientists of all originality, all talent for discovery and invention. Again, in every period, the Spaniards seriously working at science had been few; whereas to produce a Newton, an Einstein, or a Rutherford it is necessary to have a reserve of highly trained scientific workers who may never be known to the general public at all. Spain, as Cajal saw it from the stand-point of science, was like Russia before the Revolution. Apart from a devoted minority, often in exile, the majority were living mentally in the Dark Ages, 'occupied with religious legendry and political intrigue'. To one eminent Spaniard that seemed a good thing. 'Could that be called an age of ignorance and superstition, in which Spanish critics had exploded so many spurious saints, and erased their lives and miracles from the martyrologies?' Cajal might not have agreed with Menéndez y Pelayo on the value of these studies; but he refused to despair of a race 'so rich in sub-types and varieties'—one which had never ceased to produce individuals of extraordinary vigour and originality—though it had been kept back 'in a state bordering on infantilism' and prevented from reaching the full extent of its possible intellectual development. What had kept it back? One thing at least could be said. At most periods of their history the majority of the Spanish people had never been taught to read or write. Spain, as Cajal saw it, was not a degenerate country but an uneducated one, and ignorance was the result of poverty.

To Buckle, Spain seemed the country where 'the fundamental conditions of national improvement had been most flagrantly violated'. Great conquests had been made and a great military spirit developed; but progress was limited and, since it depended on a few, was unstable. In the government of the country the ruling classes were supreme and the people counted for nothing; hence the imposing edifice raised by able princes in the sixteenth century was quickly ruined by weak princes in the seventeenth. This took place along with the increasing influence of the clergy. The first use they made of their power was the expulsion of the Moslems and Moriscos, and the persecution of all Spaniards of heterodox opinions. The result was the impoverishment of Spain, decline in manufacture and population, and general decadence, material and intellectual. In regard to opinion in Spain, Buckle found the predominant states of mind to have been loyalty and superstition. He added poverty, which, with the prevalence of superstition, discouraged any attempt to think out the reasons for material things and events. The frequent famines and epidemics, instead of leading to criticism or scientific inquiry, merely confirmed habits of submission and credulity. Loyalty and reverence, he declared, had given rise to those habits of mind 'which if carried into religion cause superstition, and if carried into politics cause despotism'. In such a state of society anything approaching a secular or scientific spirit was impossible. 'Everyone believed; no one inquired.' The chief cause of decadence in politics and backwardness in science was the exaggerated development of religious and quasi-religious institutions, particularly the Holy Inquisition, which for centuries had sterilized the finest products of the Spanish mind. Those who survived were the docile and intolerant, hidebound by routine; and those who managed to express themselves were not the men of greatest intellectual ability.

This theory of the fatal effects of religious fanaticism has been supported by some of the clearest thinkers in Spain. In the nineteenth century it came to form part of the body of democratic thought which slowly spread over the country. It seemed convincing, and promised an easy remedy. Sweep away intolerance, set the critical spirit free, and the decadence would come to an end. Cajal could not deny that the exaggeration of religiosity had been one of the causes of decadence, or that the cruelties of the Holy Inquisition had helped to paralyse Spanish science. Yet he felt that the effects of religious fanaticism had been exaggerated. That was particularly the case with the effects of the Inquisition on culture. Servet (the Catalan who perceived the circulation of the blood a century before Harvey) was burnt at Geneva, not in Spain. It was not generally men of science who suffered in the dungeons of the Spanish Inquisition, but Jews, Moslems, and Protestants; and, above all, witches, who were treated barbarously in most countries in Europe in the seventeenth century. Religious intolerance could not be the only cause of decadence in Spain.

There was another hypothesis: Castilian pride. Manual labour, industry, and commerce had always been considered—among Castilians, at any rate—as low, degrading occupations unworthy of a man of birth and breeding. Pride. Snobbery. That was the disease afflicting the whole body politic. It had infected Castilians ever since they had won the war against the Spanish Moslems. Then they had expelled the Spanish Jews; but they had become themselves so filled with Judaic fanaticism that they thought themselves the Chosen People. Confusing religion with patriotism, they saw themselves achieving world-dominion beneath the banner of the Cross. But the result was isolation from the rest of Europe. The movement of ideas from which the modern world was born passed unnoticed, and Spain (Larra suggested) lost touch with modern thought by not admitting the great intellectual rebirth which had taken place in other countries after the Reformation.

This theory explains better than most others why the yield of Spanish science has been so scanty. Science needs instruments, and these can only be paid for by a flourishing commerce. Spain, yesterday the ruler, was to-day a beggar, wrapped in rags and despising everything that she did not know, as the poet Antonio Machado put it:

> *Castilla miserable, ayer dominadora,*
> *envuelta en sus andrajos desprecia cuanto ignora.*

Spain was intellectually cut off: Cajal describes it as 'spiritual encystment'. The frontiers had been closed so that the spirit of Europe should not filter through, and Europe revenged itself by erecting a moral barrier higher than the Pyrenees: a barrier of disdain. What, the eighteenth-century French intellectuals asked, do we owe to Spain? What has it ever done for Europe? And the answer was: a satirical novel, regarded as a masterpiece even to-day. In Spain there was a horror of anything new; it obsessed all teaching establishments, which became more inquisitional than the Inquisition itself, fearing and suspecting not only science, but philosophy, history, and the Greek and Latin classics. Spain had for centuries been going round in a circle, like a donkey working a *noria* (the Mediterranean water-wheel with an Arabic name), the eternal round of Aristotle and Thomas Aquinas.

There were a few exceptions to the lack of communication with the outside world. The best Spanish writers and savants were, as a rule, men who had

travelled widely, either in Europe or America:
Garcilaso, Cervantes, Quevedo; Vives, Servet, Juan,
and Alfonso de Valdés; Saavedra Fajardo, Padre
Acosta, Dr. Hernández. Occasionally some travelled
Spaniard would point out the disadvantages of the
country's isolation. Saavedra Fajardo, the political
thinker of the seventeenth century, says somewhere
that 'Renovation gives perpetuity to things which are
by nature transient.' A youth never showed his best
if he always remained in his own country. Away from
Spain, he would lose that roughness and narrow-
mindedness which were natural to him, that evil and
inhuman pride which ordinarily remained with those
who had never had experience of other countries.

Modern inquirers tend to look for explanations in
economics; and, as a matter of fact, economic theories
to account for Spanish decadence have been held by
Spanish thinkers for something like three centuries.
They were proposed by Saavedra Fajardo and Gracián
in the seventeenth century; by Cadalso, Campomanes
and Jovellanos in the eighteenth century; by Larra, Pi
y Margall, Cánovas del Castillo, Silvela, and Costa in
the nineteenth. All give importance to the low
fertility of the soil over large areas of central Spain,
and depopulation due to emigration and the expulsion
of Jews and Moriscos. Campomanes remarks particularly on the number of skilled artisans lost with the
expulsion of the Moriscos, which dealt a mortal blow
to manufacture as well as to cultivation. He says
expressly that the decadence of Spanish industry may
be dated from the year 1609, in which the expulsion
of the Moriscos began. Rice, cotton, sugar, silk, paper,
most of the products which Spanish economists claim

to have been first introduced into Europe through
Spain, were in the hands of Moslems, and the industries
were destroyed for centuries by the expulsion. It has
been said that Spain, from being an Arabia Felix—a
land of fairy-tale abundance—was converted into an
Arabia Deserta; and in a short time many parts of the
country were going hungry. Campomanes also recalls
how dexterous the Moriscos were in anything to do
with irrigation; even if the Romans introduced it, the
Moslems practised it, and in the sixteenth century alone
understood it. As early as 1535 the Venetian envoy had
noticed the ruined houses and dried-up gardens which
had belonged to the Moslems of Granada; while
Jovellanos admits that, except in those parts of the
country formerly occupied by Moslems, the Spanish
peasants knew practically nothing of the art of irrigation. When Góngora went to court from his own
south country with its clean, water-flushed cities, which
he so often praises, the dirt of Madrid and Valladolid
became an obsession with him. He wrote a few poems
which at first sight seem to be full of childish lavatory
jokes. They really express the contempt of a
Corduban, brought up beside the 'Great River', for
those foul, sluggish streams, and the disgust of an
Andalusian, used to Moslem plumbing, for the filthy
streets and nauseous smells of Castile.

Much earlier, the Castilian conquest had destroyed
that abundant wealth which the Moslems, by water
and labour, had drawn out of the soil of Andalusia.
Castile was the land once dominated by those Celts
who (as Strabo observed) ate butter instead of olive
oil; and this pastoral tradition survived in the Castilian
nobles who acquired the great southern estates after

the Reconquest. War and civil unrest will always encourage pasture against agriculture, because flocks can be moved about and because they leave man-power free for fighting. Sheep-grazing, with cheap, unskilled, and scanty labour, brought easy profits to the landlords at the cost of wide unemployment and a catastrophic fall of the common standard of living. Castilians had never known a general standard of living like that of the Moslem or Roman province of Andalusia. So the rich cultivated lands were covered with sheep, the watercourses disused and choked. From the late fifteenth century onwards, the nobles were attracted to the court, and seldom saw their estates or cared what happened on them. At the same time, Catalan commerce and agriculture were decaying. The two principal regions where wealth had been founded on work, and where economic progress had been joined to social prosperity, were both going to ruin. In one way, the Spanish Decadence began at the capture of Moslem Córdoba in 1236, and the political triumph of Castile was the economic defeat of Spain.

There was one other factor in Spanish decadence, more potent than any: inflation. The rise in prices was brought about partly by the treasure—silver and gold—brought to Spain from Mexico and Peru, and partly by the tricks played with the copper coinage by the advisers of Philip III and Philip IV in the first half of the seventeenth century. The rulers of Spain believed in the 'mercantilist' principles then in fashion, and thought that they ought to bring the largest possible amounts of precious metals into the country, and prevent as much as they could from leaving it. Seville held the monopoly of American trade, and all silver and gold had to pass through the 'India House', the *Casa de la Contratación*. The predominance of silver should be noted; after the discovery of the mines of Potosí (in the modern state of Bolivia) the treasure was largely silver, and not gold. It is untrue to claim that a large proportion of it fell into the hands of the English or the Dutch. There were only two occasions in the whole history of the treasure fleet when it failed to reach its destination: in 1628 when it was plundered by the Dutch, and in 1656 when the English prevented it from reaching Spain.

The Golden Age of Spain, in imports of precious metal and in monetary policy, as well as in art, literature, and music, was the sixteenth century. In money, it was also a Silver Age. But it was followed by an age of bronze; and the inflation of the bronze coinage (*vellón*) profoundly disturbed the economic life of Spain.

Ferdinand and Isabel, Charles V and Philip II, had all refused to debase the coinage, in spite of the perpetual shortage of ready money in the last two reigns, and the squandering of the wealth of Spain on the battle-fields of Europe. But in the reign of Philip III the decline in agriculture, industry, and commerce (which had already begun under Philip II) rapidly got worse with persecution; while the illusion that silver and gold from America would enrich the nation without work greatly reduced public revenues, which came to depend more and more on a purchase tax (*alcabala*) and customs duties (*almojarifazgo*). Philip III tried to make both ends meet by debasing the bronze coinage. His ministers were surprised at the rise in prices; the Cortes protested again and again, but without avail. Further inflation was decreed in 1618, and again in 1640. Copper (bronze) coins had been re-stamped in 1603 with a new value. On the outbreak of the wars in Catalonia and Portugal (1640), all copper money had to be handed in and stamped with double the value it had had before; the public went away with half the number of coins it had brought, and the Treasury imagined that it had made a handsome profit. The result was a disastrous rise in prices; and the price-revolution, begun by the arrival of quantities of silver and gold from America in the sixteenth century, was enormously aggravated by the loss in the purchasing power of copper. Successive Spanish governments tried every device known to them to achieve economic stability; but every time they inflated or deflated the coinage, prices swung wildly up or down, upsetting all their calculations. Commercial initiative was useless; it seemed hopeless to try to do any business whatever.

Silver prices in the first quarter of the sixteenth century had risen about fifty per cent; in the first half they had more than doubled. Then came the invention of the mercury amalgam process for extracting silver; and that, with the discovery of the Mexican silver mines of Guanajuato and Zacatecas, resulted in a deluge of silver which upset prices and wages and all arrangements between creditors and debtors. By 1601, the average price-level in Spain was more than four times what it had been a century earlier.[1] Madrid

---

[1] Retail prices depended on the wholesale prices at the principal fairs; and the municipalities would send a representative to the big fair at Medina del Campo to report on

suffered particularly from this economic crisis; and the luxurious court, with its Burgundian display and the fantastic etiquette which had gradually become naturalized in Spain and grafted on the homely court life of Ferdinand and Isabel, only added to the financial stringency, rather than bringing money into the town and alleviating the crisis. Philip III was persuaded to transfer the capital to Valladolid; but it returned in 1606, and the ever-increasing expenses of the court could be met only by confiscating family plate and church treasure. Spanish silver went abroad in paying for imports, which, now that the Moriscos had gone, included wheat. By 1623, bronze *cuartos* were being used more than silver *reales*; in the next twenty-five years, silver money disappeared, and, in spite of the inconvenience and weight, everything had to be paid for in coppers. People went about lugging great bags full of copper money. Spain, the discoverer of Mexico and Peru, had been driven off gold and silver.

In the eighteenth century things seemed to change for the better. Charles III, one of the few able men who have ever sat on the throne of the Catholic kings, was not only filled with ideas of benevolent despotism, but had a flair for choosing able men to be his ministers. Campomanes is a figure whom even a modern economist can respect. For nearly eighty years Spain seemed to go steadily forward. It could hardly make up for the ground lost in the seventeenth century. That could never be recovered; but it tried to catch up the rest

the wholesale price of spices and groceries. The top price in the other towns was then fixed by the municipal authorities (*alcaldes* and *regidores*) by adding to the Medina price something like ten per cent.

of eighteenth-century Europe. Improvement followed improvement. Even the Inquisition was made more reasonable; the burning of heretics was stopped; prosecutions for heresy were discouraged; and the Jesuits were expelled, as they had been already from Portugal and France.

Yet the reforms of Charles III, sweeping though they were in every department, were not enough to save the situation. Spain had had no seventeenth-century science and no eighteenth-century political thought. Charles III's reforms were themselves only *una revolución desde arriba*, 'reform from above', artificial respiration. They did not affect the classes lower down, which alone could have brought in new blood. Spain had been created as a great nation by the red-hot orthodoxy of its Renascence kings. To survive as a great nation it needed the white-hot heresy of England in the seventeenth century or of France in the eighteenth—not necessarily, or only, a heresy of religion, but a fundamental questioning of the nature of the physical world by scientists, of the basis of political power by philosophers, of the dogmas of economy by merchants, of the rights of gentlemen by men.

In 1784, France was electrified, scandalized, and stirred towards the Revolution by a play about Spanish characters, with its scene set in Seville: Beaumarchais' *Marriage of Figaro*. The story is of a Count Almaviva who tries to exercise his feudal right of sleeping with the bride of his barber Figaro on the night before her wedding, but is outwitted by Figaro and made ridiculous. It is one of the most passionately serious comedies ever written; a bitter attack on the power of a corrupt aristocracy. It was banned in Vienna for its revolutionary meaning, though Mozart was allowed to make it into an opera (with Italian words, so that the audience could not understand too much) and contrived to put the sting of Beaumarchais's satire into his music. The ironical fact is that, while France was set on fire by a play about Spain, a Spanish audience in 1784 would not have seen the point, or have been moved by the political implication. Spaniards did not yet realize that they had lost their liberties.

It would have been a different matter in 1809, after the French invasion of Spain and the meeting of the liberal Cortes of Cadiz, the first united Spanish parliament. The Peninsular War was a school of politics. It taught Spaniards that they could live without a king; it revived something of the medieval regional vigour; it led to the spread of democratic ideas in the towns and in the army: it restored the lost tradition of the Cortes. But in eighteenth-century Spain the public was completely apathetic. Government by itself cannot civilize a country. Reform from above has its limits. Charles III could not revive the political consciousness of Spain, for it had been anaesthetized by two centuries of absolutism. The government, for once, was enlightened; but the people's eyes were used to the black-out. Governmental efforts met with a reception that was typical. Many people in Madrid demanded that the Jesuits (whom Charles III regarded as the enemies of all progress and religious toleration) should be allowed to return and wear their usual dress, in order that Spain might be gladdened by the sight of those holy men. What can you do with a nation like this? Buckle asks. What is the use of reform when public opinion is set against it? In face of such obstacles, the government of Charles III was powerless; indeed its good intentions only did it harm, for by rousing popular sympathy in favour of a religious order it only strengthened what it sought to weaken. Even the Spanish Inquisition, the most barbarous institution which the evil genius of man had ever invented (until the rise of the Fascists), was upheld by public opinion. The public seemed to take no interest in reform when it was offered them, and could not take the initiative until after the French invasion of 1808. The Cortes had almost ceased to exist; it met only three times throughout the whole of the eighteenth century.

The reaction came to power when Charles III died in 1788, and was succeeded by the stout, orthodox, ignorant fool whom Goya caricatured in his portraits. It is amazing to think of the family of Charles IV complacently sitting for these deadly and accurate libels, which they had not the wit to understand. But the Spanish royal house had been through strange abysses of biology, even after the last of the Hapsburgs, Charles II, had ended his idiot reign and been put away in the *Pudridero*, the 'Rotting-room' at the Escurial, where he used to gape for hours at the stale corpses of his ancestors. Mr. Sacheverell Sitwell has given us a picture of the early Bourbons who came too late for Velázquez and too soon for Goya: their intolerable private lives, stiffened with such liturgical etiquette that the death of a wife—the only human friend these kings could have—drove Philip V to abdication and killed Ferdinand VI with a broken heart. It is a rare and grotesque picture: a family touched, like the

Hapsburgs, with imbecility; two of the world's greatest musicians, Domenico Scarlatti and the *castrato* singer Farinelli, immured for a generation to drive away the royal melancholy among the fantastic fountains of La Granja, which Philip Bourbon had built to recall his native Versailles; while outside, Spanish cities were decking themselves out in the curvets of Churrigueresque architecture and the rich colours of polychrome statues painted on gold.

Yet Spain was not ill governed, in the absolute Bourbon style, and was soon to pass over a feeble-minded heir into the strong hands of Charles III. His successor, Charles IV, however, had neither strength nor brains, nor even the artistic sensibility of his predecessors. In less than five years those about him were able to reverse the reforming policy which had taken three generations of statesmen to build up. Such was the condition of Spain at the time of the Napoleonic invasion; and it should be observed that the reforms which the French armies were trying to enforce had more resemblance—superficially, at any rate—to those of Charles III, or those of contemporary England, than to the blank reaction which was the immediate result of Wellington's victories in the Peninsular War.

It was in the colonies, not in the mother country, that the ideas of eighteenth-century France had a lasting effect. The Spanish administration had grown stiffer and slower as it passed from the centre to its transatlantic edges. Extraordinary devices had been used to smother the competition of colonial economy: vines had been rooted up in Mexico for the protection of Spanish wine, the eastern ports of America had been closed to European trade. There was a deep and swelling discontent among the landed creoles—the men of Spanish blood born in America. One of them became a leader of the rebellion against Spanish rule. Bolívar, like many of his generation, went to Paris as a young man in the first years of the nineteenth century, soon after the French Revolution. He came back with a new wine, more to be feared than the Mexican vintage, and strong enough to burst the old bottles of the Spanish government in America. By 1818 only a few islands were left of the empire of the conquistadores.

CHAPTER VII

ROMANTIC SPAIN

THE leaders of Spanish thought in the eighteenth century had ideas which were mainly French; hence came the Spanish proverb: When France sneezes Spain rejoins 'Bless you!' They were intellectual philanthropists, like the circle of Voltaire and the 'Encyclopaedia' in France. When the Revolution came, they added the Rights of Man and a tendency to free thought. A fine portrait of a cultivated, advanced, eighteenth-century Spaniard is to be found in Valera's novel, *El Comendador Mendoza*; though he lived long enough to be disillusioned with the French Revolution.

But in the nineteenth century the plain men shown in the great novels of Pérez Galdós have ideas which are generally the opposite: anti-French, anti-Revolution; much in favour of *trono y altar* (church and king) —even a throne occupied by so tortuous a character as Ferdinand VII, and an altar in a Church supported by the Holy Inquisition. Yet in Galdós we occasionally find a man who is an ardent upholder of the French, like Santorcaz in the novel *Bailén*: he has fought in the Napoleonic armies and has the enthusiasm of one who has actually been there, and served with Bonaparte himself.

The real reason why the majority of Spaniards were urged to rise against Napoleon was not that he was a foreign invader but that he represented the French Revolution. The greater number were fighting not for their independence but for the return of their king, who, as it happened, was one of the worst they ever had.

The truth is that the Peninsular War, the *Guerra de Independencia*, was in many ways a movement that was profoundly anti-liberal. It is disturbing to think that Wellington and his British regiments were fighting in Spain to re-establish the Inquisition; yet that is, in effect, what happened. Most histories of Spain declare that the fundamental motive of the rising against Napoleon was the feeling for national independence. This would be true if by national independence were meant the revival of the various regions of Spain. Local and regional sentiment has always been as strong as national feeling, if not stronger; and it is a mistake to read twentieth-century European national feelings into a country like early nineteenth-century Spain, where local patriotism, in spite of the centralizing policy of Hapsburgs and Bourbons, has always been so powerful and so persistent. It was the several peoples of the different regions, and not the central authority (no longer in existence), which carried on the war against the French invaders. Each region set up its own *Junta* or council, which went on with the war independently of the others, and sent representatives to treat with Wellington and even with the Government in London. There was nothing new or surprising about this; it has happened all through Spanish history whenever the central authority has broken down: it happened in 1521 with the Revolt of the Boroughs, and with the Republics of 1873 and 1936. In medieval times it was a state of affairs that was normal. The different regions took charge and carried on by themselves. How far the conventional explanation of the Peninsular War is mistaken in its interpretation of contemporary Spanish feeling can be seen from the

fact that when, a few years later (1823), another French
army invaded Spain, it met with no popular opposition.
On this occasion it was sent, not by a revolutionary
France, but by a clerical France acting for the Holy
Alliance. Its object was to sweep away the dangerously
subversive, liberal government made possible by the
pronunciamiento of Colonel Riego (1820),[1] and to
abolish (for the second time) the Constitution of Cadiz
of 1812. The invaders considered themselves to be
taking part in a crusade; and in Spain they were nick-
named 'The Hundred Thousand Sons of St. Louis'.

Spain, which had had no seventeenth century and
no eighteenth century in the ordinary European sense,
was to have no nineteenth century either. Instead of
an Industrial Revolution, there were festering agrarian
problems—a different problem for every region; instead
of imperial expansion, an empire lost; instead of
Romantic poetry, second-rate bombast and some first-
rate satire; instead of a rising parliamentary democracy,
a kaleidoscope of military dictators, who became a stage
type and left little that was permanent, except the stuff
of historical novels: the *Episodios Nacionales* of Pérez
Galdós. The generals and their cabinets swung
backwards and forwards between liberalism and
conservatism. This has been called the swing of the
pendulum in Spanish politics; it was really more like
a game of ping-pong, at which the Spanish people
looked on or, more often, turned their backs. The

---

[1] *Pronunciamiento* is the name given to the typically
Spanish military *coup d'état*. Colonel Riego's lively and
inspiriting march, the *Himno de Riego*, afterwards became the
national anthem of the Spanish Republic, instead of the
Royal March based on a flute composition attributed to
Frederick the Great.

game sometimes involved them in civil wars or in imperial adventures, but it was never their game; it did not make them richer, or teach them to read, or to govern.

Romantic politics made one side of the Spanish counterpart of the Romantic movement. At a time when the rest of Europe was becoming interested in the 'romantic' backwardness of Spain, Spaniards were beginning to demand the new romantic culture from abroad, in literature, art, music, and even in theology; though the formation of romantic taste was due not only to literary influences from abroad but also to unrest and revolution at home. Among its causes were the atrocities of the French invasion, the treachery and oppression of Spanish rulers, the economic chaos, and the desperate social conditions resulting from a long war and the loss of a great empire.

The new feature in the Spain of Espronceda and Larra (which was also the Spain of George Borrow) lay in the growth of political idealism and social consciousness. It was not a question of how far writers and artists were involved in politics, but of how their awareness of political and social conditions sharpened their sensibilities. The year 1830 was marked in the annals of Spanish Romanticism by the Byronic poet Espronceda risking his life at the barricades in Paris for his political beliefs. In Madrid, as soon as the savage tyranny of Ferdinand VII had come to an end (1830), poets and dramatists, from their café near the Teatro Español, led an enthusiastic movement in favour of Queen Cristina, who was acting as Regent for Isabel II. She had come from Naples, and had relatively progressive ideas in politics. She had also founded a

Conservatoire of Music, and encouraged Italian opera;
and one of the first direct Spanish contacts with
European Romanticism was made through the operas
of Rossini.

As the European Romantic movement gathered
momentum in Spain it brought in another favourite
-ismo of the literary historians: *costumbrismo*, the
picturesque of everyday Spanish life. Its most vivid
exponent was Larra, the best Spanish writer of his
time, a formidable satirist and one whose social
consciousness keeps his writing alive to-day. Larra
was *afrancesado*—pro-French, or even Frenchified—
by origin, education, habits, and interests. He was
born in 1809, during the French invasion; and his
father, who was an army doctor and served in the
Napoleonic war, had to leave Spain when it was over
and had his son educated at a French school. Yet he
knew the weakness of a young generation forced to
transplant its intellectual roots to France :

'At the end of the eighteenth century there was
in Spain a youth which was less apathetic and more
studious than the youth of previous generations had
been. But it was a younger generation which, when
it turned its eyes backwards to find models and masters
among its predecessors, saw nothing but an immense
void. So despairing were they of picking up the
broken threads and of continuing a movement
paralysed two centuries earlier, that they thought they
could do nothing better than leap into space, jump over
the gap, and join the movement of their neighbours
over the border, by adopting their ideas just as they
found them.'

For Larra, with his French education, the word

Spain, the concept Spain, meant an absence of order, logic, clarity, method, exactness, and rapidity. His writings, towards the end of his life, show an increasing sense of exasperation—with the plays he saw at the theatre and with the social and political conditions of Spain. He felt that in every article he wrote he buried an illusion or a hope. He was a religious man, more or less: religious enough to have religious doubts; and he is sometimes included in the history of Spanish heresy. He actually declared that Spain had missed much by keeping out of the Reformation, and he felt a sympathy for that kind of religious romanticism which produced a new current of heretical individualism, a questioning of faith by free inquiry. The Roman Catholic Church of his time was identified politically with the avenging, conservative restoration. Larra however was influenced by a more poetical Catholicism, more like that of Lamartine in France: an historical force which reached back behind the French Revolution to the libertarian, humanitarian ideals of the Gospels. Yet there was a little cloud which overshadowed this sunny, romantic religiosity: contemporary philosophy. Against the quiet mind sought by the new romantic faith stood English scepticism, the disbelief of the French Encyclopaedia, and German rationalism. This state of mind resulted in what was, for Larra, the most tragic of all states of mind: doubt.

So Larra's work is the monologue of a doubter, the soliloquy of a man unable to understand, or quite accept, the ordinary workaday world against which he has to struggle. It was, he said, a melancholy and despairing solo: 'One couldn't even write for one's own people. Who was there to listen to one? The multitude, indifferent to everything, brutalized, useless to the country for many years to come, because it had no intellectual needs and lacked all stimulus, unable to move for itself and waiting until it would allow itself to be moved. Or again, the middle class, gradually becoming more enlightened, beginning to have intellectual needs; beginning to realize that it had been, and was, in a very bad state, and desiring reform, because change was the only way by which it could better itself. Finally there was a privileged class, not very numerous, brought up in, and dazzled by, foreign parts: the victim of political emigration—a class which believed that it alone was Spain, and was surprised, at every step, to find that it was only a hundred yards in front of the rest.'

His first readers could appreciate his cleverness in getting round the censorship, his adroit allusions to the discomforts of life in that unfortunate, if romantic, epoch. Possibly they did not realize the permanent quality in his writing: his sudden vision (like Goya's); his piteous or sarcastic imagery There is the bibulous manservant on Christmas Eve, who becomes for Larra an image of Truth. There is the vision of Bilbao, starving through the Carlist siege, but raising to her famished lips a bunch of blood-stained laurel.

Spain, Larra says in another essay, was a country of *quasi*: 'almost' or 'not quite'. 'The great word nowadays, the word which applies to everything, is the word *quasi*.' That word was the whole essence of the Spanish nineteenth century. There was always something missing, something that was 'not quite'. In Spain, the leading nation of the Peninsula (that is, Quasi-island), there were certain quasi-institutions recognized by not quite the whole nation. The country was generally—not quite always—ruled by men who were quasi-mediocrities. There was still a hope, which was almost but not quite certain, that some day they would be free; but unfortunately there were too many men who were not quite competent at their jobs, while a sort of enlightenment, *una quasi ilustración*, was spreading over almost the whole country. Everything, in fact, was almost, but not quite, ready: canals not quite finished, a theatre not quite open, a palace not quite built, a museum not quite arranged, a hospital not quite in working order. This was how Larra saw Spain: the Spain of those picturesque romantic customs, that *costumbrismo romántico*, so much admired by certain writers in other countries. It drove Larra to despair, so that he shot himself. Romantic legend, of course, invented a woman in the case, and she may well have been the last straw. But it was at bottom the *quasi* of 'living and partly living' in romantic Spain that made Larra shoot himself, because he saw no other remedy.

The most romantic, the most absurd, and the most tragic movement of the time was Carlism: the faith of those who supported the claim to the crown of Don Carlos, brother of Ferdinand VII. Ferdinand had had four wives but no male heirs: the Carlist opportunity arose from a doubt whether a woman could succeed. The Cortes had set aside the Salic law and thus allowed the succession to go to a woman. Ferdinand had revoked this, but there was reason to believe that he had subsequently revoked his revocation. Traditionalist and clerical elements, supporters of an absolute, theocratic monarchy on a seventeenth-century pattern, took advantage of the turn of events to begin a civil war which went on for seven years. Queen Cristina faced the situation with courage. She signed an amnesty, allowing the exiled liberals to return from France and England, and they gave her their support. Packed in their carpet-bags they brought back two ideas, two -*ismos*, which were practically interchangeable: *romanticismo* and *liberalismo*. Their return was marked by the first performance of Spanish romantic plays which afterwards became the libretti of famous operas by Verdi. Opera was at the back of everybody's mind in those days, as the cinema is now.

Cristina's elder daughter, Isabel II, succeeded to the throne at the age of three. She was just eleven years younger than Queen Victoria; but no greater contrast could be imagined between their lives and their surroundings. Spanish romanticism is shown less in literature than in politics; and its politics were those of the bedchamber and the private chapel, combined with a passion for intrigue, violence, and speculation. One of the Queen's earliest experiences had been an attempt to carry her off from the palace by a dashing young cavalry general and two or three platoons of infantry. The grand staircase was defended all night by eighteen halberdiers and their colonel. Yet such direct attacks were less dangerous than the normal procedure of the palace. Isabel was at first the willing tool of the plotters and then their apt pupil. At the age of thirteen she lent herself to a plot which drove a prime minister (Olózaga) into exile and brought down a government. The young Queen was apparently induced to make a serious charge against the premier: that he had bolted the doors of her apartment, and then, by physical violence (catching hold of her dress and seizing her hand), had forced her to sign a decree to which she objected. The story was obviously a fabrication: the doors had no bolts. Olózaga persisted in his denial, while the Queen held by her declaration, adding that she and the minister had parted on friendly terms, and that she had given him a box of chocolates for his daughter. Chocolates lay about on all the chairs of the palace. When Isabel was asked about the incident years afterwards she was uncertain what had happened about the decree, but she was quite sure about the chocolates.

The King-Consort's name was Don Francis of Assisi. From his high, squeaky voice he was known as Paquita—'Fanny'. From a doubt in some diplomatic circles as to whether he was capable of becoming a father, he was selected by the high policy of France as a suitable husband for Isabel; and at the same time Isabel's sister was married to the Duc de Montpensier, who was to supply a French heir to the Spanish throne. Isabel upset all these ingenious schemes. To the consternation not only of the French diplomats but of her husband she produced a son. 'Fanny', who suffered from the odd delusion that the child was not his, had to be restrained from informing the chancelleries of Europe to that effect, and from demanding a dissolution of the marriage. As time went on, he counted a family of nine.

Isabel never really grew up. She had a good heart and generous instincts, but she was never queen over her passions. 'A safe word whispered by a crawling confessor,' an American diplomat remarked, 'an

attack of nerves on a cloudy day, the appearance of a
well-made soldier at a levee, have often sufficed to
make and break administrations.' Behind the throne
stood Father Claret, the Queen's confessor, and Sor
Patrocinio, the Bleeding Nun, in whose hands and
feet were the marks of the wounds of Christ. The
stigmata were discreetly veiled from view by mittens;
yet there is reason for believing that the wounds were
self-inflicted, and the wax-white, mittened fingers
were in every pie. Her power over the Queen was
incalculable. On at least one occasion she upset a
ministry for no apparent reason, and brought the
Crown into ridicule. Pérez Galdós, in the historical
novel *Prim*, has described a scene which actually took
place in 1865:

'Suddenly, when no one was expecting it, the
government fell. *Quare causa?* Why? No one knew;
and what was worse, no one asked. We had become
accustomed to governments coming and going for no
other reason than the whims and fancies of the Señora.
That lady was certainly confused and embittered just
then by the news brought from Paris by the King-
Consort who had been to pay a visit to the Empress
Eugénie. Napoleon and his wife had given him a
dressing-down for the obstinacy with which Spain
refused to recognize the new kingdom of Italy, a *fait
accompli* which no country in Europe could consider
as non-existent and remain within the comity of
nations. The conduct of Spain was intolerable
quixotism. This, more or less, was what they had
said to Don Francis of Assisi; and in the same form
as they had urged it upon him he passed it on to his
spouse. She, however, raised her hands in horror,

repeating in a trembling, frightened voice: "But we can't! We *can't*!"

'Isabel II communicated immediately with her guardian angels Sor Patrocinio and Father Claret, reporting the dire communication which Don Francis of Assisi had brought from Paris. It is reported that both reverend personages pursed their lips and knitted their brows. Let Napoleon rule in his own house and leave our gracious Queen to govern in hers! Spain should remain firm in her decision relating to the so-called kingdom of Italy, and with the protection of the Virgin she had nothing to fear from the concert or disconcert of Europe. . . .

'She summoned the minister in attendance.

'"Narváez."

'"Señora?"

'"I want you now, more than ever. I have dismissed the Government. Make me any ministry you like; I don't mind what you do so long as it doesn't involve the recognition of Italy. . . ."

'Narváez took the helm of the leaking ship of state.

'Some little apologies for elections were held. . . . But . . . it wouldn't do. Narváez must go. She came to this conclusion two days before the opening of the new Cortes : and as she thought, so she did, offended and mortified. Narváez had decided on the evacuation of Santo Domingo, the only possible way out of a long and expensive war. . . .

'"Istúriz."

'"Señora?"

'"Narváez has deceived me; I must do without him. Besides, I do not agree to the evacuation of Santo

Domingo. You will form me a ministry with unionist elements. . . ."

'"I, Señora, *I* . . . ?"

'The illustrious old man who had served the Spanish monarchy so well, both in politics and diplomacy, hesitated between his respect for the Queen and his dislike of lending himself once more to such pastry-cook's work in public. . . . But the excuses with which his modesty and weariness would have eluded the task were of no avail; her exquisite amiability and the sweetness of her manner overcame him.

'"Not at all. Not at all. I ask you this as a favour and you are not going to deny me. To-morrow, at this time, you will bring me the list of your ministry."

'When the twenty-four hours were past, good old Don Javier arrived at the palace with the list of the new ministers.

'"Are they all there? Let's see. . . . Good. I agree. What time is it? Twelve? Well, at three o'clock punctually they may come and take the oath."

'But by a quarter to three she had changed her mind.

'"Istúriz."

'"Señora?"

'"That's all settled. Narváez has been here, and oh! what things he told me! But we will leave all that for another time."

'Leave it for another time! He breathed again.'

The Portuguese were in the habit of referring to Queen Isabel's Spain as the madhouse over the border. Spanish political history in this period was a comic opera in which every act ended in tragedy; and in 1868 (as in 1931) there were many who favoured revolution, not because they were anti-monarchist but because they were anti-Bourbon. They saw what the surroundings of Spanish royalty had become, and the strength of the 'traditional obstacles'. *Esa Señora*, that lady, had become impossible.

The *coup d'état* of General Prim and the dethrone-ment of Isabel II came in 1868. Father Claret and Sor Patrocinio disappeared. The provisional govern-ment offered the crown of the Catholic kings to all the royalties within reach. Queen Victoria hastened to declare that no member of her family should touch it; and the rumour that it was to be offered to a Hohen-zollern was one of the immediate causes of the Franco-Prussian war of 1870. Finally the choice fell on the Duke of Aosta, Amadeo of Savoy: but he soon found Spain too cold for him.

The First Republic, proclaimed in 1873, never had a chance. A flaw in its origin incapacitated it from the beginning. It was born of Cortes that were monarchist at heart and centralist in ideas; yet its supporters in the country were federalist. Though not discussed in the Cortes, federalism was tried in the provinces; the different regions immediately came to life, and turned themselves into independent cantons. But the experiment failed, and the various cantons were forcibly suppressed by the centralist government in Madrid. It was many weeks, however, before the canton of Cartagena fell; and before the year was out the Republic itself had fallen before a general and a *pronunciamiento*, while the monarchy was restored at the end of 1874 by another *pronunciamiento* under another general. A second Carlist war added to the confusion.

With the Restoration of the Bourbon Monarchy in

1875, Liberal and Conservative ministries alternated in regular succession. But it was only a shadow of parliamentary government: the alternation became known in Spain as 'the Changing of the Guard', which exactly expressed this revolving show of parliaments around the Royal Palace which made and broke them. Further military adventures in Cuba and the Philippine Islands led to the Spanish-American war of 1898, and the loss of all that remained of the Spanish Empire.

CHAPTER VIII

MODERN SPAIN

SPANISH history seemed to have got into the state of an old gramophone record when the needle keeps slipping back into the same groove at the same point, each time it revolves. After the Restoration of 1875 only one man saw and took a way forward, out of the illusory gyration of politics, towards real progress. He was not a politician, but a Professor of Law at the University of Madrid. Don Francisco Giner de los Ríos was the first modern Spaniard: it would be invidious to call him the greatest, in a period of unusual and varied brilliance; but more than any other man he gave to Spain the impulse which set it moving, and which it must recapture in some form if it is ever to move again.

Don Francisco [1] saw that reform from above, by politicians, had no lasting effect. Charles III had failed because the Spanish people had been too long kept out of political activity to understand what he meant. The suppression of the Cortes of Cadiz and the fall of the First Republic had plunged them into apathy again; there was an uneasy and critical minority, but, as President Castelar said, one generation could not make a revolution twice. The fundamental need was to educate men and women to take their place in society—not least, the governing classes. From

---

[1] 'Don So-and-so' (with the Christian name) is not a special title; it is the way Spaniards address each other in all classes. Giner is commonly spoken of as 'Don Francisco' by all who learned from him, or admired him.

bottom to top, the nation must be taken to school; and the first thing it had to find was a group of men fit to become its tutors.

Don Francisco's conception was, however, nothing like the courses in 'Education for Citizenship' which we hear of in England: Spain needed something more elementary and at the same time more ambitious. He was not concerned with applying ideas to politics, but with creating the ideas themselves, the ferment of pure speculation and the passion for knowledge which had long been extinct in the country. Those who cry for more 'practical' forms of education—whose reaction to a grammar-book is like Isabel I's: 'What is it for?'—might do well to study Spanish history and see how the decline of academic learning slows down the vital processes of a people, stunts their economic growth, makes them hungry and sick and backward. Don Francisco's answer was reading and writing, history and mathematics, philosophy and science. He was attacking the problem at source.

The first thing that happened was that he was expelled from his university chair by the government. With a few friends, he founded the Free Institution for Education (*Institución Libre de Enseñanza*), a preparatory and secondary school which became the greatest stimulus in the rebuilding of the Spanish mind. Reactionaries—if they were shrewd enough—feared it more than social revolution; yet it taught no specific social doctrines. It was 'a home of peace, new ideas, and mutual respect'. It never at any time received official support, and refused to be associated with any political party. Don Francisco annoyed the traditionally minded by his unusual and un-Spanish behaviour: he seemed un-Spanish in his rejection of party politics, and 'protestant' in the modesty of his approach. He was never put off by the argument that a plan formed part of a much larger question and had better wait until the whole could be dealt with adequately—a line of reasoning which has prevented much from being done in Spain. His own plan was not to produce legislation—the time was not ripe for that—but to train up the legislators of the future, to give them a new outlook by which they could guide the country. He had no definite system or scheme of education which could be handed over to a government department and introduced by decree throughout the country; no ready-made article to be sold to a dictator and put on the market. His ideas were quietly put into practice with the help of his friends. It was a prolonged experiment, a direction, an aim, a reform that was never finished.

Building beyond the stage of his model school for boys and girls, his friends founded the *Residencia de Estudiantes* and the *Residencia de Señoritas*, university colleges on the pattern of Oxford and Cambridge, with lecture-rooms and laboratories, and the *Centro de Estudios Históricos* for higher studies. The body which watched over all these activities, the *Junta para Ampliación de Estudios*, was administered by one of Don Francisco's ablest and most far-sighted disciples. Another friend, M. B. Cossío, the art historian, carried forward his plans on the wider scale which was taken up as a policy by the Second Republic of 1931. Cossío's ideal, to bring the university to the elementary school, was realized not only by college-trained teachers but also by lay missions, mostly of university men, bringing

painting and music, books and plays, to the most
remote and forgotten villages of Spain—some of them
so mountainous and inaccessible that the 'missionaries'
were warned not to go there: people seldom died a
natural death, they were told, but fell over the edge.
They went there all the same, bringing their books and
paintings on mule-back or on their own shoulders.
Books. Cossío was never impressed by the devout
philistinism which proclaims illiteracy a state of grace,
and more particularly a saving grace of the Spanish
people. The essential thing was to teach people to read
books. That was the core of the Spanish problem:
read, possess books. With these pioneers behind it
the Second Republic—whatever its other mistakes—
knew what it was doing in education. It had no time
to train enough teachers to fill the schools it built, but
even in the midst of civil war its efforts went on, in
new schools just behind the lines, in special courses at
hospitals or barracks, in printing presses which turned
out books in the trenches themselves. As families
were broken up, more people wanted to read and write
in order to get news of their relations; workers saw
that books opened the way to technical knowledge; but
there was also a real hunger for learning in itself. The
small beginnings of Don Francisco Giner had spread
to millions, though no time was left for achievement.

The *Institucionistas* themselves always remained a
minority, but to their life and work are due the best
things that have come out of Spain in a century: not
only in education but in science, scholarship, and art.
At a time when the clerical Right wing in Spain
opposed all scientific teaching as a carrier of moral
infection; when the great physiologist Ramón y Cajal

had to learn anatomy by secret body-snatching; when degrees could be got by memorizing text-books or even by bribing the examiners, the pupils of Don Francisco were felt like the breath of a Renascence—as indeed they were. For the first time since Philip II young Spanish scholars were wandering freely about Europe —or as freely as their poverty permitted; and at the same time their eyes were being opened to the great things of their own country. *The Times* correspondent in the eighteen-seventies remarked that 'boys of twelve at the Institution possess a knowledge, for instance, of architectural styles that some architects might envy, gained by repeated visits to the most noteworthy buildings in Spain'.

It was this revival of interest in Spain and Spanish things that most clearly influenced the political thinking of the day. The influence was indirect, for Don Francisco was no sectarian. With some of the ideals of a socialist and others of an anarchist, he acted in the faith and optimism of a liberal. He was never on the side of the big battalions, either Right-wing or Left, and he loathed vulgarity. Democracy, if it was limited to voting at elections, was an imperfect instrument, and the oppression of a minority by a majority he regarded as iniquitous. His experience had left him with 'a melancholy distrust of any rapid influence on the multitude and confirmed him definitely in the belief that the only honourable or possible course lay in the slow preparation of the men of the future'. But twenty years after he had begun his work came the war in which Spain lost Cuba and the Philippines: the last shreds of her American empire. It was the end of that mirage overseas for which Spaniards had lived in squalor in their own land; which had drained their population and wrecked their economy. The disillusionment turned their eyes inwards, and the more thoughtful minds among them discovered the Spain at home, with its landscape, literature, and art, which Don Francisco had been showing to his pupils.

Many of this group, indeed, were themselves pupils of Don Francisco, and all of them had felt his ideas in some way. They have become known in Spain as the 'Generation of '98'. From their discovery of Spain they drew not merely comfort in past achievements but hope and plans for the future. The Empire was gone, and a good riddance; now was the time to make Spain habitable for Spaniards. There were no facilities for doing anything, Pío Baroja complained. We must lock and double-lock the sepulchre of the Cid, said Joaquín Costa; we will swap glory for progress and battleships for schools. Costa declared that the country did not need the blood of heroes and martyrs so much as *sangfroid*, brains, self-control, mutual good-will, and, above all, enough to eat. His ideas of reform were radical and drastic: he wanted, for instance, to abolish the Spanish fleet and to transform the whole social system of upper Aragon, where irrigation was impossible and a patriarchal tradition kept alive hopeless agricultural misery and incurable family hatreds. Costa was himself the son of an Aragonese labourer, and no more likely than most of the Generation of '98 to sentimentalize the Spanish peasant. His methods were drastic too: he was a passionate liberal who advocated dictatorship— though this was to be, like the dictatorships of the Roman Republic, an elected office, strictly limited in time. Don Fernando de los Ríos has told how Costa

one day found an old Spanish poem beginning:
'Castile seemed a province that had been laid waste;
and its towns, fields without cultivation; the soldiery
naked, the nobility barefoot, the people beggars; all
action cramped.' He showed it to Don Francisco,
saying: 'Giner, that is Spain.'

'No, Joaquín,' Giner answered; 'that was Spain.
Spain is different now.'

'Giner, we want a man.'

'Joaquín, what we want is a people.'

In the circumstances of the time, the Generation of
98 could take no direct action in political reform,
though they represented all that could be called political
thought in Spain. They were writers, poets, scholars,
artists, and musicians—the first of that remarkable
flowering of the Spanish mind which was suddenly cut
down in 1939. There was Miguel de Unamuno, the
greatest personality of them all, who is known abroad
chiefly for his book, *The Tragic Sense of Life in Men and
Peoples*. He was also a novelist, a poet, a gigantic
walker, Professor of Greek at Salamanca, then an
exile in Paris, until his devastating invective had helped
to blast the dictator Primo out of Spain. Unamuno
was larger than his writings. He once quoted Walt
Whitman: 'I charge that there be no theory or school
founded out of me'—as if any theory or school could
balance upon the vehement discords, the clash of
antinomies and contradictions, which to Unamuno
were the life-essence of thought.

There was Ramón del Valle-Inclán (y Montenegro,
he fantastically tacked on to his name), who was
inspired by the romantic anachronisms of the Carlist
movement to his best creation—himself: a twentieth-

century Byron in exquisite Castilian prose. There was the novelist Pío Baroja; the new light-shod style of Azorín's essays; and the massive historical scholarship of Altamira and Menéndez Pidal. The barrier of the Pyrenees was beginning to break down: Ortega y Gasset brought German philosophy to Spain; Ramiro de Maeztu interpreted the life of England; Manuel Cossío rediscovered El Greco for Europe. Sorolla and Picasso, Miró and Dalí, were renewing the Spanish tradition of painting; and in Catalonia music began again with Pedrell, Albéniz, Granados, and then the magical violoncello of Pau Casals. But the greatest composer was an Andalusian, Manuel de Falla. It was a shock, among the antics of the 'Armistice School' of music in Paris, to hear a man who could use his orchestra as brilliantly as Stravinsky, writing serious music with the movement of a race of dancers and the incisiveness of the guitar, the wit and the sharp tragic quality of southern Spain—for Andalusia is a tragic land.

In Granada, the new music and the new poetry sometimes met. On summer nights, in the gardens, there would be a party beside the fountains and the demijohns—*damajuanas*—of native sherry; Falla would be there, with a trio of plucked instruments playing his music; a young man who was born near Granada was asked to recite his own poems—his earliest poems, which were as unmistakably written for plucked strings as Elizabethan songs. This was Federico García Lorca. It is hard to make any account of his work sound credible to ears which are used to the strenuous thinking, and the deliberate avoidance of sensual effects, in modern poetry outside Spain. Lorca, like Lope de Vega, made the Spanish ballad and the folk-song into modern things, and the Spanish verse-drama as well. It was possible, in Andalusia in the nineteen-twenties, to write without any romanticism of gypsies and knives and horsemen, because they were there all the time in ordinary life: they were no more exotic than the Civil Guard, the brutal police, who run like a red thread through Lorca's gypsy ballads. It was possible to be 'popular' without being 'proletarian', or showing any consciousness of class. Lorca's poetry is highly wrought and not facile, but it comes out of him like the blood of his gypsy Antonio Torres Heredia, 'in a fountain of five jets'. Being a painter and musician as well, he had singular sensual faculties, and his poetry is full of violent imagery which he later intensified into a deliberate surrealism. A short early song is here quoted, for its Andalusian awareness of death and fate. Mr. Stephen Spender's translation keeps the assonant o-sounds of the traditional Spanish form:

> Córdoba.
> Far away and alone.
>
> Black pony, big moon,
> and olives in my saddle-bag.
> Although I know the roads
> I'll never reach Córdoba.
>
> Through the plain, through the wind,
> black pony, red moon.
> Death is looking at me
> from the towers of Córdoba.
>
> Ah! How long the road!
> Ah! My valiant pony!
> Ah! That death should wait me
> before I reach Córdoba!
>
> Córdoba.
> Far away and alone.

Federico García Lorca was shot in Granada by Right-wing gunmen, in 1936, when he was thirty-seven. After the two authentic, neglected voices of the nineteenth century—Bécquer and Rosalía de Castro—Spanish poetry had been shaken into life by a gifted Nicaraguan, Rubén Darío, who had mixed his literary drinks in France. Many poets came after him and reacted away from his exuberant style. Antonio Machado was an Andalusian whose first lyrics inhabited the 'secret tunnels' of the mind and its dreams; later, he emerged from them to look at the land of Castile with a portrait-painter's vision, and with a passion like Costa's. He died in France as a fugitive, during the exodus of the Republicans from Catalonia. Juan Ramón Jiménez, the most exquisite craftsman of modern Spanish poetry, went to live and write in America; the finest of the younger poets, Cernuda, came to England, like the best of the new composers, Gerhard.

This was the modern Spain that was dispersed in 1939. Very few of its distinguished men remain in their own country. Those who think only of the political analysis miss the life of the story: Spain had more to lose than a government. Don Francisco Giner had often asked what was to become of Spain:

'The best men die without leaving any to come after them. There is a generation or two of intelligent people. Then comes a political catastrophe, and we have to begin all over again. If only we could profit by what we have already! But we are so deeply divided between Catholics and Liberals, right wing and left, that one half can never profit by the knowledge and achievements of the other.'

The movement led by Don Francisco and the

Generation of '98 had not penetrated Spanish politics. In spite of the growth of popular political consciousness, the 'traditional obstacles' still remained; and in matters of government there was no real change from the customs of the nineteenth century. Some of the governments were called Liberal; some of the nineteenth-century military dictators were also called Liberal. The term, in politics, meant little more than anti-clericalism and the repeal of what the last government had done; Liberalism, as we understand it, was developing outside the political game, among such men as Don Francisco and Costa. Perpetual *pronunciamientos* had weakened respect for constitutional forms; and it was not restored, in the intervals between dictators, by the Cabinet shuffles of King Alfonso XIII, a clever politician whose abilities were wasted on the technique of manipulating parliaments from inside the palace, far removed from the real forces which were stirring in the nation. It was, indeed, hard for the successor of so many Hapsburgs and Bourbons to establish contact with his people. In spite of the lessons which thoughtful men had drawn from the loss of Cuba, the government was spending money and conscribing levies for its imperial adventures in Morocco. A resounding defeat in 1923, due to the impatience of the king and the carelessness of a commander, brought heavy casualties with bitter resentment at home. The situation was patched up once more by the dictatorship of a general. Costa had once said that what Spain needed was an 'iron surgeon'. General Primo de Rivera (as Unamuno commented) was more like a quack dentist. He was an energetic builder of roads, telephones, harbour installations, and other useful gadgets, but he had no understanding of the social and political question: Spain, under his management, presented the appearance of a Renascence play in modern dress. The next general gave way before a decisively anti-monarchist vote in municipal elections, and the king left Spain peacefully in April 1931, in a cruiser of the Second Spanish Republic.

The problems which the new Republic was called upon to solve were delicate and deep-seated. Three lost centuries came shooting to the top; nothing had been thoroughly or finally settled for so long; it was almost as if England were confronted all at once with the deferred conditions of the Reformation, the Commonwealth, and the repeal of the Corn Laws, at a time when the Irish question was burning and modern social doctrines were spreading among the workers. These parallels are not, of course, intended to be exact; but Spain was facing no less fundamental changes. And they had to be faced by parliamentary methods in a country where parliamentary parties, through long disuse or abuse, were not the most powerful forces in political life.

In the end, the internal conflict of Spain was invaded and overlaid by an international conflict. Internationally, it was not hard to understand, either as an incident of European strategy or as a struggle of ideologies, in which millions of people outside Spain saw a picture of their own hopes, prejudices, or fears. But the Spanish conflict itself was nothing so simple. It began a long way back in the past of a country where conditions were unique, and where political labels seldom meant what they mean in the rest of Europe. Even when we know what the labels mean, we do not know much about modern Spain. When we speak of politics, we must remember that many Spaniards were ignorant of them, or uninterested or divided in their own minds. When we speak of groups or movements, we must remember that Spaniards do not easily sink their individual selves in membership of a group. They are, as Strabo said, 'bad mixers' in the political sense, though sociable enough in private. Most of them will escape any system of pigeon-holing. A Spanish Anarchist or Falangist will not behave like all the other Anarchists or Falangists in Spain: he will not really try to. Yet, among a people so difficult to organize, those organizations which do exist gain an advantage, and can wield uncommon power. To form some idea of the situation, it is necessary to consider the various bodies which were powerful in Spain during the Republic.

The Army in 1931 was more suitable for use in Spain than abroad: it had an extraordinary proportion of officers and a great many generals. The higher ranks had never had enough professional occupation to keep their minds off politics, while junior officers could not live on their pay. For over a century the weakness of the civil authority had tempted ambitious generals to indulge in *coups d'état* in the national style. They had got into the habit of 'saving Spain' on every possible occasion; and while they often ruled no worse than the politicians of the monarchy, their interventions were temporarily upsetting and permanently damaging to constitutional government. The Army had become to all intents and purposes a political party—indeed, the most stable political party in Spain. The Republic of 1931 took the heroic course of retiring all supernumerary officers on full pay, which looked fair enough. But it threw upon the country a large group of self-appointed statesmen with a grievance, an independent income, and nothing to do except to intrigue in clubs for their return to influence.

Next, there was the question of land-owning. Liberals, labourers, and afterwards Falangists, agreed that the conditions of work on the large estates were intolerable. It was not only that wages were disgracefully low. The day-labourer had no security of employment—not for any reason connected with his own efficiency, but because the landowner might decide any day to turn over his estate to hunting or sheep-farming, and discharge his workers in hundreds. In the South, a few owners held nearly all the land, and their freedom to use it as they liked was not limited by the economic good of Spain any more than by its social welfare. In Catalonia, a country of smaller estates which are leased to tenant-farmers, the tenant could be dispossessed on the spot if he fell short of his yearly payment in kind. The payment was usually excessive for the times, and in a bad year more than a thousand tenants might be turned out. In north-west Spain tenants were oppressed by an ancient system of seignorial dues, and were constantly in debt; the men emigrated when they could, and unmarried women were left to work the tiny fields. Beneath it all there were long-standing Spanish evils: depopulation, and the lack of scientific research, engineering technique, and industrial development, which were necessary to irrigate the dry lands or manure the thin soil of the plateau, and to balance economic life.

The Republic raised wages. The landowners

promptly changed over to pasture and sacked their
employees. The Republic distributed land to labourers.
The Socialists (for good reasons) contested this, in

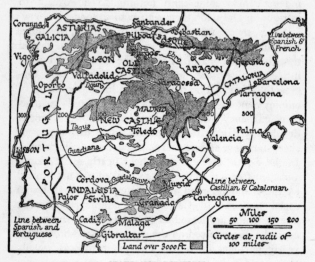

SPAIN AND PORTUGAL
(*from* J. M. Thompson's *Historical Geography of Europe*)

favour of collective tenure. The Catalans drew up a
Bill settling their own tenant-problem. The land-
owners stirred up a Conservative tribunal in Madrid
to quash the Bill. In the end little was done. The
plan of land-distribution was carried out in a few
districts: in others it was neglected, sabotaged, or
misunderstood (for instance, a Castilian peasant owner,
working a small holding with one farm hand, might
come down one morning and find his farm hand

claiming to expropriate him, as if he were a great landlord like the Duke of Medinaceli). Misunderstandings
were not always the fault of the Republican administration; nevertheless, its ignorance of agriculture
exasperated labourers as well as landowners. It never
really grasped the fact that Spain needed not one
agrarian policy but four or five, with sub-types and
variations. Its officials arrived from Madrid by car
and told the farmer things they had read in books.
Spaniards who do not farm with their own hands—
even if they live in the country—sometimes show an
indifference to natural objects which would amaze a
Cockney. The landlords, who were mostly absentees,
are seldom any better. Though the first general
policy of the Republic had been well conceived, it was
wrecked by this combination of vested interests on the
one hand and departmental ineptitude on the other.

The bitterest controversy of all was concerned with
the Church. Outside Spain it is not always realized
that this controversy was more ecclesiastical than
religious: that is, that many Spaniards who wanted to
restrict the activities of the Church were not atheists
but believing Catholics. From the early nineteenth
century there had been outbursts of popular anti-
clericalism, with violence and church-burnings, but
this behaviour did not originally spring from any
definite political or philosophical theories. In the
twentieth century Spain had a fairly strong minority
of atheists and agnostics, but there was a large number
of anti-clerical Catholics. Such anti-clericalism was
rare in some regions—in the Basque country, for
instance, or Catalonia—where the Church had been
better served by its ministers. In fact, what was

resented was not the Catholic faith but the power and intolerance of the clergy in matters outside religion.

Historically, the Spanish Church was hardly a typical Catholic body, in spite of its religious orthodoxy. It had been transformed into something like a national Church by the Renascence monarchs, who had fought against the Pope on occasion, and had exacted unusual privileges of ecclesiastical independence. In the political sphere, the kings had used the Church as an instrument and the Church in its turn had used the kings. This was common enough in Europe at the time. But most other countries have long ago passed through a struggle between Church and State, from which the Church has emerged weaker in political power, though it may have recovered its spiritual influence. In Spain and Spanish America, however, the struggle has been delayed, without reaching any clear conclusion until quite recent times, or not even then. These lands, owing to their lack of education, were scarcely touched by the various reformist or rationalist philosophies which were fashionable at different times in the rest of Europe. Further, their governments usually had less organizing ability than their churches, which took on many of the functions performed in other modern nations by private companies or the State.

The Spanish Church had been forced to sell its lands in the nineteenth century, and although it had acquired other investments, and a State subsidy, its wealth was by no means so monstrous as some writers have declared. The priesthood and the monastic orders were very large, but were mostly poor men, underpaid and ill-educated. The Church had, however, wide connexions with business enterprises, owned a number of newspapers, and also possessed a great system of banks and syndicates which supplied credit and collected crops all over the countryside of Castile. It had organized these syndicates when there was nobody else to do the job, and it managed them efficiently, by Spanish standards of private business. But its various lay concerns gave it great influence, which it often used in an intolerant manner. The statement that it is a sin to vote Liberal occurs in a Catechism published as late as 1927; and the same edition condemns Darwinism, freedom of education, and the unrestricted right of meeting and propaganda. Some Spanish priests held more enlightened views (Catalonia, in particular, had some fine brains and some noble characters among its clergy), but the majority were ignorant and averse to social or intellectual progress.

It was not surprising that the Republic of 1931 thought this Church unfit to run the schools of the nation, or to exercise even its limited control over university appointments. The Jesuits had some good schools, but they also had some bad ones, and the disgraceful level of Spanish education was enough to condemn the system. While it lasted, there seemed no prospect of improvement. But whether the Liberals were wise in their legislation of 1931 is another question. The power of the Church had to be curtailed in many directions, but it was rash to make a frontal assault, tactless to season it with doctrinaire sentiments, and over-hasty to sweep away the entire system of Church schools for uniformity's sake, before anything was completely ready to take their place, instead of remembering the precept of Don Francisco Giner: 'If you find a bad school, leave it alone and open a good school opposite.' The men of 1931 had energy, they had ideas, and they had excellent aims, but they had not always the political skill to carry out those aims in the most prudent way.

The question of the Monarchy was much less acute. Outside court circles only a few stalwart Galicians wanted to restore Alfonso. But the Carlists, defeated in two nineteenth-century wars of succession, were still vigorous, and quite unruffled by the fact that the Pretender for whom they had fought was long ago forgotten. They now claimed to be the party of Tradition. Their policy was to put the clock back— but not further back than the seventeenth century. Earlier history would scarcely have recognized their ideal State ruled by King and Pope. Carlism was popular in a few districts, especially in the intransigent land of Navarre, whose bitten limestone mountains enclosed a patriarchal society of magnificent fighters. Its political programme had little chance of conquering Spain in peace, but during the civil war it gained strength from the value of its forces in the field, the red-capped Requetés.

All these elements were openly or covertly ranged against the Republic on the Right wing. They were reinforced in the nineteen-thirties by new groups whose ideology came from Italy. Like the early Fascists and Brownshirts, these had radical ideas on land reform and social services, and they demanded the subjection of all private interests to a corporative authoritarian State. Their various groups coalesced in 1934; but up to the outbreak of the civil war they were still small in numbers, though noisy and ready with their rifles. They were the nucleus of the later Spanish Phalanx.

There were also forces ranged on the Left of the Liberal parties. Up to 1936, the Communists were as few as the Falangists. The pretence that the National-ist rising forestalled a Communist plot is not supported either by evidence or probability. Communism is too disciplined a doctrine to appeal to most Spaniards, and it gained ground only when, during the civil war, it adopted anti-revolutionary tactics aimed at keeping order among the wilder groups, who were more interested in violent social change than in winning the war.

The strongest of these revolutionary parties was Anarchism. It has been called the Left-wing form of Carlism, which it resembled in its curious indifference to modern economic progress and its visionary attitude to society. It was the Arcadian creed of a people which, through centuries of misrule, had lost all faith in governments. The State was the root of all evil; the natural perfection of man was expressed in local units—the village, the factory, or even the battalion— making their own decisions by acclamation, on a system of 'organized indiscipline' which rejected the iniquity of centralized or external control. The effects of this doctrine on the battle-field were unsatisfactory, but it reveals the primitive and abiding faith of the Spanish people in the only political institution which they had been allowed to create for themselves: the Iberian city council, driven back, since the decay of medieval municipal liberties, into the remote villages of the South. Andalusia was the home of this purer

form of Anarchism, where a passion for equity and
simplicity went with the almost Oriental patience of
men who had lived too long below the poverty-line to
care any more about material improvement. Among
the factory workers of Barcelona, Anarchism was only
the inner core of a more modern, energetic movement:
Syndicalism, which had been introduced into France
by Sorel, and involved the control of industry by
workers' corporations. But Anarcho-Syndicalists, too,
were less preoccupied with economic improvement
than with the austere religion of the Russian Anarchist
Bakunin, naturalized in an intensely Spanish form.
They were, in their way, puritans. They broke
up sacred images with the fury of fanatics, and
closed the night-clubs of the *Barrio chino*, the Red
Lamp Quarter of Barcelona. Many of them were
teetotallers and vegetarians: they would gravely
discuss whether it was allowable to eat steak before
going 'over the top', or which was the most humane
way of killing an enemy. Such characters seem out
of place in the cultured, businesslike democracy of
Catalonia; but for the most part they were not Catalans.
They came there to get employment, from the hot
African landscape of Murcia in the south-east.

The 'Socialist' or trade union movement was as
strong as anarchism, but it represented the more
practical temperament of the industrial workers in
Madrid and the North. It supported the first Liberal
government of the Republic; then, when a Conservative government came to office, half the trade
unionists turned towards revolutionary methods. The
other wing stuck to its constitutional line of action.

The strength of these parties must not be exaggerated. Spain has little industry, and the agrarian workers were scattered. Large masses of the population, in the country or the small towns, accepted political events with varying degrees of content or indifference. But the traditional obstacles and the extreme Right- or Left-wing doctrines were sufficiently formidable to a new Liberal Republic—though Spanish Liberalism, too, was a formidable thing. As we have seen, it had been denied expression through the government of the country, and had developed outside professional politics, in the sphere of culture and ideas. The commercial middle class of Spain was too weak to have given it that powerful economic basis on which English Liberalism was built. Yet to call it mere abstract intellectualism would be a profound mistake. It had concentrated in itself all the long discontent of the country; it had found and spoken the only words for the desire to change. The Spanish Liberals were the spearhead of modern Spain.

A minority of this kind was as dangerous as dynamite under the dictatorship or the monarchy. But in office, as the Government of Spain, it began to feel the disadvantages of being a minority and of having no direct political experience. It inherited not only a bad parliamentary tradition but a civil service of uncommon corpulence and inefficiency. More serious than any of these handicaps was the fact that not all the Republican parties wanted extensive reform. The Second Republic was by no means an uninterrupted experiment in progressive liberalism. Its five years of peace were equally divided between the Liberals who started off in 1931, with a series of great achievements and grave mistakes, and the Conservative (Centre-

Right) government which followed them in 1933, and reversed or obstructed their legislation.

Of the Liberal achievements, one of the most promising was the settlement of the Catalan question. Since the political subordination of Aragon to Castile in the fifteenth century, and the economic decay of the east coast after America was discovered, Catalonia's condition had gone from bad to worse. The seventeenth-century kings had overridden the Catalan *fueros* and repressed the province by force of arms. In the war of the Spanish Succession Catalonia had allied itself with England in return for a guarantee of protection; but England abandoned it after the war to the vengeance of Philip V, and Barcelona had been sacked in 1714 by the Duke of Berwick. Speaking its own language, maintaining its own customs, it had seen this language and these customs banned by the centralist Castilian monarchy and finally by Primo de Rivera. While its money was taken in taxes and its men conscripted in war, its songs and even its folk-dances were considered subversive. Catalonia has been called the Irish problem of Spain: a comparison which would be apt if Ireland were a hard-working, progressive, and wealthy country, much superior to England in education and in the development of its industry. Catalonia objected to making money for the common use of a nation which it regarded as backward and feckless. The Basques were in much the same case, and had been treated almost as oppressively. They are a stubborn race of sailors, farmers, and merchants; they are capable in industry, stout Conservatives, and for the most part firm Catholics.

A people whose gift for local self-government has

been proved again and again in its history, and frustrated again and again by an incompetent central authority, will always come forward at critical moments to take charge of its own affairs in village, province, or town. But this action, which recurs in almost every crisis of Spanish history, is spontaneous and spasmodic. It should be distinguished from the larger and more permanent regional movements whose mainspring is nationalistic.

A stranger entering Spain from three out of the four points of the compass finds himself among people whose speech is not 'Spanish'—or, more accurately, not Castilian. If he arrives by the north he will hear a language unlike any other in the world: Basque. If he arrives by the east he will hear a language something like French Provençal: Catalan. If he arrives by the west he will hear a language like Portuguese: Galician. All these peoples have been ruled for centuries from Castile, a land of unquenchable adventure and supreme imperial talent, springing from the barrenness of its own soil. Castile made Spain what it has been in history, but it has constantly dragged down a higher standard of living on its margins. In one region it stamped out a whole culture and wrecked an economic life; that was in Moslem Andalusia, the fourth point of the compass. Elsewhere, its rigid domination has exasperated national feelings which might have been fruitful and innocent. The Basque and Catalan nationalist movements are the two most highly organized expressions of protest; but similar parties of varying importance exist in almost all of the lands which encircle the Castilian plateau. In both regions there was ardent agitation for Home Rule. This was granted in Catalonia soon after the Republic was established, and the new free state set about solving its agrarian problem in a liberal and sensible way—which was more than the rest of Spain had done. When its Land Bill was thrown out in Madrid, Catalonia seceded, was crushed, and lost its autonomy. The Liberals restored it in 1936, and also gave Home Rule to the Basques.

The Right wing, which embodies the Castilian political tradition, is strongly opposed to every form of Home Rule; and Spanish Socialists also regard the subject with suspicion. What is certain is that in a land of such various geography and tradition—a land of four distinct languages, apart from dialects— political unity cannot be attained by ignoring differences. Regionalism may go too far: Spain could not survive a relapse into its medieval fragments, and it is perhaps impracticable to adopt Pi y Margall's oracular nineteenth-century formula of 'a synallagmatic, commutative and bilateral federalism', which hardly anybody except himself understood; but at least the policy of 'Castilianization' has been proved a failure three centuries stale. Spain needs a flexible, well-informed administration, carefully balanced between central and local authority, such as the Peninsula has not known since Roman times.

During the five years before war broke out there were two foretastes of catastrophe. In 1932 a general staged a *pronunciamiento* in Seville, and was defeated without much trouble. In October 1934 the trade unionists of Asturias revolted against the inclusion of Right-wing ministers in a Cabinet of the Centre parties; Catalonia seceded at the same time; a local and miniature civil war ensued, and the rebels were harshly suppressed. This incident revealed the fatal contradiction inside the State. On the one hand, the Right had emerged from the last elections as the biggest *bloc* in Parliament: it was entitled to seats in the Government by the constitutional rules of a democracy. On the other hand, this same Right wing was bitterly opposing reforms to which the Republic was committed by the articles of its Constitution. Whether the Right was loyal to Republican principles at all was not beyond doubt: its leaders may have been, but it included men whose records are not reassuring—for instance, Ramón Serrano Suñer. The old question had arisen: Can democratic privileges be accorded to people who may use them to overthrow democracy? But in the ultimate event, no Spanish party really built its case upon the constitutional correctness of its behaviour, nor yet upon that 'right to rebellion' which is also known to political philosophy. Such ideas have little meaning except as they apply to the actual situation, in the country and at the time; and they were used chiefly in argument for foreign consumption. The Spanish crisis must be judged in other terms: in terms of the history of Spain.

The elections of 1936 brought a sweeping victory to the parties of the Left, though on a proportional count of votes the majority was no bigger than that of the British Conservatives in 1935. But the danger lay not so much in the evenness of the voting as in the heavier loading of the extreme wings, both Left and Right. There was much disorder, and in July a group of high Army officers rebelled in typical nineteenth-century style. The gramophone needle had slipped again. But in 1936 the results were very different. On earlier occasions the mass of the people had never taken much notice of *pronunciamientos*: they looked on and waited for the next. This time the Army's stroke was balked by strong popular opposition. The rebels had planned a lightning change between midnight and breakfast: instead they had to fight for nearly three years.

The time has not yet come to write a history of this war, nor of what followed. Too much is unknown which may some day be accessible to students, and judgement is still confused by the abuse of victory and the bitterness of defeat. Meanwhile, the behaviour of a people engaged in fighting one another is neither typical nor very instructive—not, at least, for the purpose of a study of their civilization. Both sides went through considerable changes in the course of the struggle, and Spain emerged under the leadership of a general, with a new official party called *Falange Española Tradicionalista y de las Juntas de Ofensiva Nacional-Sindicalista*.

When peace broke out (as both sides put it) many Spaniards were dead, many more in prison or in exile. Half Spain was starving, and the rest was soon to go hungry too; the fields were uncultivated, cities had been bombed to pieces. The new springs of vitality, which had been rising in such abundance during the last forty years, were choked and poisoned by war. Mere physical survival seemed uncertain, and progress was hardly to be thought of. It was a picture like the old poem which Costa had shown to Don Francisco, with the same question appended: '"Giner, we want a man." "Joaquín, what we want is a people."'

Englishmen are apt to turn with some impatience

from the history of modern Spain, and many Spaniards,
too, have come to regard their country as inherently
and irremediably lacking in the political virtues.
Compromise, moderation, constitutional stability are
not unjustly praised in our own country, but Spain
has shown little of these in recent times. We forget,
perhaps, that such qualities are the product of a settled
and well-knit State; they are not impossible to develop
once this State is established, and they are necessary
to keep it in health; but they will not, by themselves,
be enough to create it from its painful or bloody
beginnings. We now look back on the seventeenth
century as not the least admirable period of our
English history. At that time, when Germany was
commended by Cervantes for its liberty of conscience,
England had 'an unsavoury reputation for swinging
between violent political extremes'. That is the
reputation of modern Spain; but it was not always so.
Pliny once wrote of Spain to a friend, saying: 'That
province, as you know, has great judgement, great
sense of responsibility'; and again during the Middle
Ages Spaniards showed their political talent in their
townships and parliaments. For the future, whatever
else may happen to Spain, the lesson of Don Francisco
Giner is still waiting to be learnt. When Don
Francisco died the poet Antonio Machado, his pupil,
found words for his message:

'Is he dead? All we are sure of
Is this: the path he took lies clear before us.
He said: "I want no mourning;
Remembering me by work and hope is better. . . .
He who leaves work well done is with us still,
And he who truly lived lives on.
Let anvils clash for me, and bells be silent." '

BIBLIOGRAPHY

GENERAL

THE indispensable history of Spain and Spanish civilization is R. Altamira, *Historia de España y de la civilización española* (4 vols., 4th ed., Barcelona, 1929). It has a bibliography and an alphabetical index. The *Compendio de historia de España* by Aguado Bleye (1932) and the large illustrated history by Ballesteros y Beretta (9 vols., Barcelona, 1919–36) are also useful and provided with bibliographies.

These notes refer mainly to books in English. There is no complete translation of Altamira. The *History of Spain founded on the 'Historia'* . . . *of Rafael Altamira* by C. E. Chapman (New York, 1918) omits many aspects of Spanish civilization. The *History of Spanish Civilization* (London, 1930) is an English translation of Altamira's *Historia de la civilización española* (Madrid, 1928), not an extract from the larger work in four volumes. It is finely illustrated and has an excellent bibliography. Shorter historical summaries will be found in David Hannay, *Spain* (London, 1917), and W. C. Atkinson, *Spain: a brief history* (London, 1934). The *History of Iberian Civilization* by J. P. de Oliveira Martins (Oxford, 1930) lost some of its point and brilliance in translation. A modern psychological study is *Englishmen, Frenchmen, and Spaniards* by S. de Madariaga (Oxford, 1928); some of the *Essays and Soliloquies* of Miguel de Unamuno may be read in an English translation (London, 1925), but Altamira's *Psicología del pueblo español* (Barcelona, 2nd ed., 1917) has never found a translator.

The history of the language is dealt with by W. J. Entwistle, *The Spanish Language* (London, 1936). The most reliable history of Spanish literature is the English translation of Ernest Mérimée, revised and enlarged by S. Griswold Morley (New York and London, 1931). *A New History of Spanish Literature* by James Fitzmaurice-Kelly (Oxford, 1926) is also available. The field of A. F. G. Bell's *Castilian Literature* (Oxford, 1938) is more restricted.

The fine arts in Spain are admirably reviewed in the *Burlington Magazine* publication, *Spanish Art* (London, 1927), which includes architecture, painting, sculpture, textiles, ceramics, woodwork, and metalwork, and gives useful bibliographies. *Catalan Art from the 9th to the 15th Centuries* (London, 1937) is superbly illustrated. Sir Charles Holmes, in *Old Masters and Modern Art* (vol. ii, London, 1925), described the Spanish pictures in the National Gallery. The most thorough study of the subject is *A History of Spanish Painting* (7 vols., Harvard, 1930–38) by C. R. Post. Illuminated manuscripts are described and illustrated by J. Domínguez Bordona in *Spanish Illumination* (2 vols., Paris, 1930), translated by Bernard Bevan.

The *History of Spanish Architecture* by Bernard Bevan (London, 1938) is thoroughly up-to-date and well illustrated. The pioneer work in English on *The Industrial Arts in Spain* was that of Juan F. Riaño (South Kensington Museum, 1879); *Hispanic Lace-making* has been described by Florence L. May (Hispanic Society of America, 1939); *The Regional Costumes of Spain* by Isabel de Palencia (Madrid, 1926).

Riaño was responsible for another pioneer work,

Critical and Bibliographical Notes on Early Spanish Music (London, 1887); while numerous references to Spain, relating music to social history, are to be found in P. H. Láng, *Music and Western Civilization* (New York and London, 1942). *Manuel de Falla and Spanish Music* by J. B. Trend (New York and London, 2nd ed., 1935) deals mainly with the later periods. Kurt Schindler's *Folk Music and Poetry in Spain and Portugal* was published after his death by the Hispanic Institute in New York, 1941. The latest book on the subject in English is *The Music of Spain*, by Gilbert Chase (New York and London, 1943).

Spanish gardens are shown by Mildred and Arthur Byne, *Spanish Gardens and Patios* (Philadelphia and London, 1924), by Helen M. Fox, *Patio Gardens* (New York, 1929), and C. M. Villiers-Stuart, *Spanish Gardens* (London, 1929).

English books on Spanish travel are innumerable. George Borrow's *Bible in Spain* is a classic which deserves its reputation. Richard Ford's *Handbook for Travellers in Spain and Readers at Home* (2 vols., London, 1845) is inimitable, though cut down in every later edition. It is a mine of information on 'antiquities, religion, legends, fine arts, sports, and gastronomy, with notices on Spanish history'. Standing apart from all other books is Gertrude Bone's *Days in Old Spain* (London, 1938), with magnificent illustrations from drawings by Sir Muirhead Bone.

The best bibliography of Spain is J. Fitzmaurice-Kelly, *Spanish Bibliography* (Hispanic Society of America, 1925). A useful guide is the *Subject Index of the London Library* (3 vols., 1909–38).

CHAPTER I

An authoritative study of *Fossil Man in Spain* was made by H. Obermaier (Hispanic Society of America, 1924). The standard work on Peninsular ethnology is that of P. Bosch-Gimpera (Barcelona, 1932); originally published in Catalan, an abridged Spanish version is being prepared in Mexico. *Hispania*, by A. Schulten and P. Bosch-Gimpera, is an enlarged Spanish edition of the article in Pauly-Wissowa's *Real-Encyclopädie*. The *Essai sur l'art et l'industrie de l'Espagne primitive* by Pierre Paris (Paris, 1903–4) is a classic. *The Iberians in Spain* by Pierson Dixon (Oxford, 1940) is a short, readable book with good illustrations, the only one so far available in English. The Greek and Latin sources for the classical period have been collected by A. Schulten and P. Bosch-Gimpera in *Fontes Hispaniae Antiquae* (4 vols., Barcelona, 1922–37). *The Greeks in Spain* by Rhys Carpenter (Hispanic Society of America, 1925) is brief but fascinating, while *The Romans in Spain* by C. H. V. Sutherland (London, 1939) is a short text-book which stops unaccountably at A.D. 117. *Wars of Ideas in Spain: Philosophy, Politics, and Education*, by José Castillejo (London, 1937), discusses the Spanish-Romans Seneca and Quintilian as educators. In *The Cambridge Ancient History*, see vol. vii, ch. 24: The Carthaginians in Spain; vol. viii, ch. 10: The Romans in Spain; vol. xi, ch. 12: The Latin West. These chapters have bibliographies.

CHAPTER II

The *Encyclopaedia of Islam* (4 vols. and suppl., Leyden, 1908–38) is the best authority, in English, for the Moslem peoples in Spain. Dozy's *Spanish Islam* (English translation, London, 1913) is a brilliantly written account of the earlier period. The standard work in English on Arabic literature is *A Literary History of the Arabs* by R. A. Nicholson (2nd ed., Cambridge, 1930); it has special reference to the Arabic prose and poetry written in Spain. A brief manual is *Arabic Literature: an Introduction*, by H. A. R. Gibb (Oxford, 1926); the Spanish contribution is carefully noted. *The Legacy of Islam*, edited by Sir Thomas Arnold and Alfred Guillaume (Oxford, 1931), includes chapters on Islamic arts and their influence, in Spain, and the Islamic view of society. Important, for Islamic thought in Spain, is D. B. Macdonald, *Development of Muslim Theology, Jurisprudence, and Constitutional Theory* (New York, 1903); the scientific contribution of Moslem Spain is appraised by Charles Singer in *A Short History of Science* (Oxford, 1941). Miguel Asín Palacios in *Islam and the Divine Comedy* (London, 1936) shows the influence of Moslem Spanish mysticism.

Islamic architecture in Spain is considered in relation to that in other parts of the Islamic world in G. T. Rivoira, *Moslem Architecture: its origins and development* (Oxford, 1918), and E. T. Richmond, *Moslem Architecture* (London, 1926). The famous 'Hispano-Moresque' lustre pottery is included in the *Burlington Magazine* volume on Spanish art (already mentioned). A. F. Kendrick's *Catalogue of Muhammadan Textiles of the Medieval Period* (Victoria and Albert Museum, 1924) illustrates splendid fragments from Spain. The end of Spanish Moslem civilization is described by H. C. Lea, *The Moriscos of*

Spain: their conversion and expulsion (Philadelphia, 1901).

The Jewish factor in medieval Spanish thought is brought out in *The Legacy of Israel*, ed. Edwyn Bevan and Charles Singer (Oxford, 1927). The daily life of the Jews in Spain is shown in *The 'Responsa' of Rabbi Solomon ben Adreth of Barcelona* (London, 1925). The philosophy of Maimonides is expounded in *Spinoza, Descartes, and Maimonides*, by Leon Roth (Oxford, 1924), and in *Papers connected with the 8th centenary of his birth* (London, 1935). Hebrew elements in medieval Spanish culture are described in *Abravanel: six lectures with an introductory essay*, ed. H. Loewe and J. B. Trend (Cambridge, 1937). Isaac de Costa gives an account of *Noble families among the Sephardic* [Western] *Jews* (Oxford, 1936). The latest account of the expulsion, in English, is that of Valeriu Marcu, *The Expulsion of the Jews from Spain* (London, 1935).

CHAPTER III

A general account of the period is to be found in R. B. Merriman, *The Rise of the Spanish Empire*, vol. i: The Middle Ages (New York, 1918), and in the *Cambridge Medieval History*; the medieval Spanish Cortes are described in vol. vii, ch. 23, and in the *History of Medieval Political Theory in the West*, vol. vi (Edinburgh and London, 1936), by A. J. Carlyle. *The Cid and his Spain*, by R. Menéndez Pidal, is a compressed English translation from the larger work in Spanish. Guy le Strange in *Spanish Ballads* (Cambridge, 1920) gave a selection in historical sequence with a valuable commentary; later research

on Spanish romances was included by W. J. Entwistle
in *European Balladry* (Oxford, 1939).

The Catalan contribution can be seen from H. J.
Chaytor, *A History of Aragon and Catalonia* (London,
1933); a shorter sketch of Catalan culture is included
in J. B. Trend's *Picture of Modern Spain* (London,
1921). *The Chronicle of Muntaner* was translated for
the Hakluyt Society (1920–21) by Lady Goodenough.
The Catalan language is illustrated and explained
(with examples from early chroniclers to the writers of
to-day) by J. L. Gili, *Catalan Grammar with a historical
outline of Language and Literature* (Oxford: Dolphin
Book Co., 1943).

Early medieval Spanish art is exemplified by W. M.
Whitehill, *Spanish Romanesque Architecture of the
11th Century* (Oxford, 1941), and A. Kingsley Porter,
Spanish Romanesque Sculpture (2 vols., Paris, 1928).
Street's *Gothic Architecture in Spain*, first published in
1865, was reprinted in 1914. Gustave Reese, *Music
in the Middle Ages* (New York and London, 1941),
incorporates the most recent research on early Spanish
music.

CHAPTER IV

For the reign of Ferdinand and Isabel, see R. B.
Merriman, *The Rise of the Spanish Empire*, vol. ii
(New York, 1918). Among recent studies of Columbus
are those of S. de Madariaga (London, 1939), support-
ing the theory of his Jewish origin, and S. E. Morison
(New York and Oxford, 1942), following the Admiral
as a navigator. C. H. Haring, *Trade and Navigation
between Spain and the Indies* (Harvard Economic
Series), shows how navigation to America developed

in the following reigns. The lives of Spanish explorers are described by F. A. Kirkpatrick, *The Spanish Conquistadores* (London, 1934). *Central and South America, 1493–1913,* by W. R. Shepherd, forms a separate volume in this series (Home University Library, 1914). One of the earliest humanists in Spain, Lucio Marineo Siculo, is the subject of *A College Professor of the Renaissance,* by Caro Lynn (University of Chicago Press, 1937). Nebrija's Spanish Grammar has been edited with an introduction in English by I. González Llubera (Oxford, 1926). Foster Watson translated *Vives on Education* (Cambridge, 1913).

For the Emperor Charles V the main authorities are: Edward Armstrong (2 vols., London, 1910); R. B. Merriman, vol. iii (New York, 1925), and K. Brandi, translated by Veronica Wedgwood (London, 1939). The *Comunero* movement of 1520–21 has been investigated by H. L. Seaver, *The Great Revolt in Castile* (Cambridge, Mass., and London, 1929). This and the following reigns occupy *The Golden Century of Spain, 1501–1621,* by R. Trevor Davies (London 1937).

Philip II is best studied in R. B. Merriman, vol. iv: *Philip the Prudent* (New York, 1934). *An Hour of Spain between 1560 and 1590,* by the Spanish essayist Azorín (translated by Alice Raleigh, London, 1930), is a vision of Spanish life in the time of Philip II. *The Spanish Inquisition* is the subject of another volume in this series, by A. S. Turberville (Home University Library, 1932).

Spanish political thought in the sixteenth century has no better exponent than A. J. Carlyle (see under Chapter III). His *Political Liberty* (Oxford, 1940) has been translated into Spanish and published in Mexico (1942). J. B. Scott has described Francisco de Victoria as the first international lawyer: *The Spanish Origin of International Law* (Oxford, 1926); J. H. Parry has studied *The Spanish Theory of Empire in the 16th Century* (Cambridge, 1940). In this connexion, the two lectures by Fernando de los Ríos should be read in *Concerning Latin American Culture*, ed. Charles Griffin (New York, 1940). S. A. Zavala's work on the ideas of Sir Thomas More as they affected a Spanish colonial judge are to be found (in Spanish) in *La 'Utopia' de Tomás Moro en la Nueva España* (Biblioteca histórica mexicana de obras inéditas, 1937), and in *Idearío de Vasco de Quiroga* (Mexico, 1942).

The history of Spanish printing is given by K. Haebler, *Early Printers of Spain and Portugal* (Bibliographical Society, 1897); Sir Stephen Gaselee, *The Early Spanish Printing Press* (London, 1924); Henry Thomas, *Spanish 16th-Century Printing* (London, 1926) *Early Book-illustration in Spain* was published in 1925 by J. R. P. Lyell. Dr. Thomas has also produced a standard work on *Early Spanish Bookbindings* (Bibliographical Society, 1939), as well as the *Short-title Catalogue of Books printed in Spain . . . before 1601* (British Museum). A *List of Books printed before 1601 in the Library of the Hispanic Society of America* was published in 1929.

CHAPTER V

The bibliography of Cervantes will be found in *Cervantes: a tentative bibliography* by J. D. M. Ford and Ruth Lansing (Harvard and Oxford, 1931).

Modern interpreters of Don Quixote (Unamuno, Madariaga) are apt to set up a figure of their own, rather than the one created by Cervantes. W. J. Entwistle's *Cervantes* (Oxford, 1940) is a more sober study. A. F. G. Bell, in *Luis de León* (Oxford, 1925), gives the intellectual background of the whole epoch.

The influence of Erasmus has been admirably treated by Professor Bataillon, *Érasme et l'Espagne* (Paris, 1937). *The Spanish Reformers* by Edward Boehmer (2 vols., London, 1874–83) is still authoritative; Juan de Valdés and the Valdesian movement have recently been described in English by G. K. Brown, *Italy and the Reformation to 1550* (Oxford: Blackwell, 1933). The best modern work in English on the spiritual history of Spain is *The Other Spanish Christ*, by John A. Mackay (London, 1932). The few pages on mysticism in Spain included in W. R. Inge's Bampton Lectures, *Christian Mysticism* (1899), are still the most satisfactory introduction to the subject in English, with the works of Baruzi (in French). E. Allison Peers has also dealt with the subject. The place of mysticism in Spanish poetry is discussed by Pedro Salinas, *Reality and the Poet in Spanish Poetry* (Baltimore and Oxford, 1940).

The bibliography of the Spanish stage will be found in any history of Spanish literature. Recent additions are the chapter on the Spanish religious theatre in *17th-Century Studies presented to Sir Herbert Grierson* (Oxford, 1938), and *The Allegorical Drama of Calderón* by A. A. Parker (Dolphin Book Co., 1943). The dramatic art of Calderón is related to the painting of El Greco and the Baroque style in architecture and opera. An introduction to the painter, in English, is *El*

Greco, by Frank Rutter (London, 1930); this, like the larger and more pretentious books, owes a great debt to the pioneer research of M. B. Cossío. The relation between El Greco and the Baroque style seems first to have been pointed out by Roger Fry, *Vision and Design* (London, 1920, and in Pelican Books, 1937). The *Baroque Architecture* of Martin Shaw Briggs (London, 1913) included a chapter on Spain and Spanish America; but English interest in the subject was really aroused by Sacheverell Sitwell, *Southern Baroque Art* (London, 1924), with its vivid studies of painting, architecture, and music in Spain and Mexico in the seventeenth and eighteenth centuries, and *Spanish Baroque Art* (London, 1931). The lectures of W. Weisbach, *Spanish Baroque Art* (Cambridge, 1941), ignore the colonial aspect.

CHAPTER VI

In the extensive literature of Spanish decadence two works stand out. H. T. Buckle's *History of Civilization in England* (1857–61), with its long chapter on the Spanish intellect, was revised by J. M. Robertson in 1904. The views of Ramón y Cajal are included in his 'Rules and advice on scientific research': *Reglas y consejos sobre investigación científica* (6th ed., Madrid, 1923); reprinted in Buenos Aires as *Los tónicos de la voluntad* (1941). The most convincing exposition of the economic causes is that of Earl J. Hamilton, *American Treasure and the Price Revolution in Spain, 1501–1650* (Harvard Economic Studies, 1934). J. O. McLachlan has studied the trade-conditions in *Trade and Peace with Old Spain, 1667–1750* (Cambridge, 1940).

Social life in the reign of Charles III is revealed by the *Travel Diaries of William Beckford* (new ed., London, 1928). Goya's attitude to Charles IV is brought out by Lord Derwent, *Goya: an impression of Spain* (London, 1930). Manners and customs are illustrated by Charles E. Kany, *Life and Manners in Madrid, 1750-1800* (University of California Press, 1932).

CHAPTER VII

There are a number of manuals of nineteenth-century Spanish history (e.g. Martin Hume, Butler Clarke), and the chapters in the *Cambridge Modern History*. More understanding is shown in the brief references to Spain in the *History of Europe in the 19th Century* by Benedetto Croce (English translation, London, 1934), and by H. A. L. Fisher in *The Republican Tradition in Europe* (London, 1911); while the matrimonial arrangements of Isabel II and her sister have been investigated from the standpoint of foreign policy by E. Jones Parry, *The Spanish Marriages, 1841-46* (London, 1936).

The educationists, who set about making a better Spain, are described by José Castillejo, in *Wars of Ideas in Spain* (London, 1937), and introduced into *The Genius of Spain* by S. de Madariaga (Oxford, 1923). An account of Krause and his influence in Spain may be read, in English, in *The Philosophy of History in Europe*, by Robert Flint (Edinburgh, 1874); but the more important sources for this period have not yet been translated. They are indicated in *The Origins of Modern Spain*, by J. B. Trend (Cambridge, 1934).

The romantic view is expressed by E. Allison Peers,

A History of the Romantic Movement in Spain (2 vols.,
Cambridge, 1940), and by J. L. McClelland, *The
Origins of the Romantic Movement in Spain* (Liverpool,
1937); but these works confine romanticism to questions of literary theory. A more balanced view is to
be found in *El siglo romántico*, by Adolfo Salazar
(Madrid, 1936). Marx and Engels *Revolution in Spain*
(1939) is interesting. Rhea Marsh Smith, in *The Day
of the Liberals in Spain* (University of Pennsylvania
Press, 1938), and others, rightly saw that an important
clue to modern Spain was to be found in the history
of Spanish Liberalism.

CHAPTER VIII

It is not within the scope of this bibliography to
mention books concerned exclusively with the war of
1936–39. For these, see the list in *Voice of Spain*,
No. 14, June 1941. Of special interest is J. Álvarez del
Vayo's important work: *Freedom's Battle* (London,
1942).

In a different category, for knowledge and treatment
of Spain before the war, is S. de Madariaga's *Spain*
(London, 1930; revised, 1942). Book I of this work
is an admirable study and has a good bibliography;
Book II, like most even of the serious works on the
Spanish war, is controversial. E. Allison Peers, in
The Spanish Tragedy (London, 1936), gives a narrative
of events in 1930–36 from a Conservative standpoint.
His version of the ecclesiastical problem should be
balanced with (e.g.) S. de Madariaga's *Spain*, chapter
xiii. Elliot Paul's *Life and Death of a Spanish Town*
(London, 1937) is a fine and sensitive picture of the

island of Ibiza before and during the war. *The Spanish Labyrinth*, by Gerald Brenan (Cambridge, 1943), is the only book on the conditions leading to the Civil War which historians can read with real respect. The chapters on agriculture and on the history and philosophies of the political organizations are the best things yet written on the subjects. See also the *Surveys* published by the Royal Institute of International Affairs (London, 1920–) and the *Publications* of the U.S. Council on Foreign Relations (New Haven, 1922–).

What was lost in the war was not merely a government, but a whole modern culture. In the literature of the period, some of the poems of Federico García Lorca appeared with an English translation by Stephen Spender and J. L. Gili (*Poems* : London, 1939). *Lost Angel* and other poems by Pedro Salinas have been printed in the same way, an English version facing the Spanish (Baltimore and Oxford, 1938). A selection of contemporary poetry was added to the second edition of the *Oxford Book of Spanish Verse* (1940); but the best collections of Spanish poetry in our time are the one edited by Gerardo Diego, *Poesía Española: contemporáneos* (2nd ed., Madrid, 1934), and *Laurel: Poesía moderna en español* (Mexico, 1940). Contemporary Spanish prose is represented in English versions of the more important essays of Unamuno, Azorín, Gabriel Miró, and Ortega y Gasset. References to the painting of Picasso and the music of Falla will be found in bibliographies of modern painting and modern music.

INDEX

213

PRINTED IN
GREAT BRITAIN
BY
NEILL AND CO. LTD.
EDINBURGH